Department of the Treasury

Internal Revenue Service

Publication 54
Cat. No. 14999E

Tax Guide for U.S. Citizens and Resident Aliens Abroad

For use in preparing

2015 Returns

Get forms and other information faster and easier at:
- *IRS.gov* **(English)**
- *IRS.gov/Spanish* **(Español)**
- *IRS.gov/Chinese* ( )
- *IRS.gov/Korean* (한국어)
- *IRS.gov/Russian* (Русский)
- *IRS.gov/Vietnamese* (TiếngViệt)

Contents

Future Developments

For the latest information about developments related to Pub. 54, such as legislation enacted after it was published, go to *www.irs.gov/pub54*.

What's New

Additional child tax credit. You cannot take the additional child tax credit if you claim either the foreign earned income or foreign housing exclusion, or foreign housing deduction. For more information on the additional child tax credit, see the Instructions for Form 1040.

Exclusion amount. The maximum foreign earned income exclusion is adjusted annually for inflation. For 2015, the maximum exclusion has increased to $100,800. See *Limit on Excludable Amount* under *Foreign Earned Income Exclusion* in chapter 4.

Housing expenses — base amount. The computation of the base housing amount (line 32 of Form 2555) is tied to the maximum foreign earned income exclusion. The amount is 16 percent of the exclusion amount (computed on a daily basis), multiplied by the number of days in your qualifying period that fall within your 2015 tax year. For 2015, this amount is $44.19 per day ($16,128 per year). See *Housing Amount* under *Foreign Housing Exclusion and Deduction* in chapter 4.

Housing expenses — maximum amount. The amount of qualified housing expenses eligible for the housing exclusion and housing deduction has changed for some locations. See *Limit on housing expenses* under *Foreign Housing Exclusion and Deduction* in chapter 4.

Filing requirements. Generally, the amount of income you can receive before you must file an income tax return has increased. These amounts are shown in chapter 1 under *Filing Requirements*.

Self-employment tax rate. For 2015, the maximum amount of net earnings from self-employment that is subject to the social security part of the self-employment tax has increased to $118,500. All net earnings are subject to the Medicare part of the tax. For more information, see chapter 3.

IRA limitations for 2015. You may be able to take an IRA deduction if you were covered by a retirement plan and your 2015 modified adjusted gross income (AGI) is less than $71,000 ($118,000 if married filing jointly or a qualifying widow(er)). If your spouse was covered by a retirement plan, but you were not, you may be able to take an IRA deduction if your 2015 modified AGI is less than $193,000. See the Instructions for Form 1040 or the Instructions for Form 1040A for details and exceptions.

Reminders

Figuring tax on income not excluded. If you claim the foreign earned income exclusion, the housing exclusion, or both, you must figure the tax on your nonexcluded income using the tax rates that would have applied had you not claimed the exclusions. See the Instructions for Form 1040 and complete the *Foreign Earned Income Tax Worksheet* to figure the amount of tax to enter on Form 1040, line 44. If you must attach Form 6251 to your return, use the *Foreign Earned Income Tax Worksheet* provided in the Instructions for Form 6251.

Form 8938. If you had foreign financial assets in 2015, you may have to file Form 8938 with your return. See *Form 8938* in chapter 1.

Change of address. If you change your home mailing address, notify the Internal Revenue Service using Form 8822. If you are changing your business address, use Form 8822-B.

Photographs of missing children. The Internal Revenue Service is a proud partner with the National Center for Missing and Exploited Children. Photographs of missing children selected by the Center may appear in this publication on pages that would otherwise be blank. You can help bring these children home by looking at the photographs and calling 1-800-THE-LOST (1-800-843-5678) if you recognize a child.

Introduction

This publication discusses special tax rules for U.S. citizens and resident aliens who work abroad or who have income earned in foreign countries.

If you are a U.S. citizen or resident alien, your worldwide income generally is subject to U.S. income tax, regardless of where you are living. Also, you are subject to the same income tax filing requirements that apply to U.S. citizens or resident aliens living in the United States. Expatriation tax provisions apply to U.S. citizens who have renounced their citizenship and long-term residents who have ended their residency. These provisions are discussed in chapter 4 of Pub. 519, U.S. Tax Guide for Aliens.

Resident alien. A resident alien is an individual who is not a citizen or national of the United States and who meets either the green card test or the substantial presence test for the calendar year.

1. **Green card test.** You are a U.S. resident if you were a lawful permanent resident of the United States at any time during the calendar year. This is known as the green card test because resident aliens hold immigrant visas (also known as green cards).

2. **Substantial presence test.** You are considered a U.S. resident if you meet the substantial presence test for the calendar year. To meet this test, you must be physically present in the United States on at least:

   a. 31 days during the current calendar year, and

   b. A total of 183 days during the current year and the 2 preceding years, counting all the days of physical presence in the current year, but only $\frac{1}{3}$ the number of days of presence in the first preceding year, and only $\frac{1}{6}$ the number of days in the second preceding year.

   Example. You were physically present in the United States on 120 days in each of the years 2013, 2014, and 2015. To determine if you meet the substantial presence test for 2015, count the full 120 days of presence in 2015, 40 days in 2014 ($\frac{1}{3}$ of 120), and 20 days

in 2013 ($\frac{1}{6}$ of 120). Because the total for the 3-year period is 180 days, you are not considered a resident under the substantial presence test for 2015.

For more information on resident and nonresident status, the tests for residence, and the exceptions to them, see Pub. 519.

Filing information. Chapter 1 contains general filing information, such as:
- Whether you must file a U.S. tax return,
- When and where to file your return,
- How to report your income if it is paid in foreign currency,
- How to treat a nonresident alien spouse as a U.S. resident, and
- Whether you must pay estimated tax.

Withholding tax. Chapter 2 discusses the withholding of income, social security, and Medicare taxes from the pay of U.S. citizens and resident aliens.

Self-employment tax. Chapter 3 discusses who must pay self-employment tax.

Foreign earned income exclusion and housing exclusion and deduction. Chapter 4 discusses income tax benefits that apply if you meet certain requirements while living abroad. You may qualify to treat up to $100,800 of your income as not taxable by the United States. You also may be able to either deduct part of your housing expenses from your income or treat a limited amount of income used for housing expenses as not taxable by the United States. These benefits are called the foreign earned income exclusion and the foreign housing deduction and exclusion.

To qualify for either of the exclusions or the deduction, you must have a tax home in a foreign country and earn income from personal services performed in a foreign country. These rules are explained in chapter 4.

If you are going to exclude or deduct your income as discussed above, you must file Form 2555 or Form 2555-EZ.

Exemptions, deductions, and credits. Chapter 5 discusses exemptions, deductions, and credits you may be able to claim on your return. These are generally the same as if you were living in the United States. However, if you choose to exclude foreign earned income or housing amounts, you cannot deduct or exclude any item or take a credit for any item that is related to the amounts you exclude. Among the topics discussed in chapter 5 are:
- Exemptions,
- Contributions to foreign organizations,
- Foreign moving expenses,
- Contributions to individual retirement arrangements (IRAs), and
- Foreign taxes.

Tax treaty benefits. Chapter 6 discusses some benefits that are common to most tax treaties and explains how to get help if you think you are not receiving a treaty benefit to which you are entitled. It also explains how to get copies of tax treaties.

How to get tax help. Chapter 7 is an explanation of how to get information and assistance from the IRS.

Questions and answers. Frequently asked questions and answers to those questions are presented in the back of the publication.

Comments and suggestions. We welcome your comments about this publication and your suggestions for future editions.

You can send us comments from www.irs.gov/formspubs. Click on "More Information" and then on "Give us feedback."

Or you can write to:

Internal Revenue Service
Tax Forms and Publications
1111 Constitution Ave. NW, IR-6526
Washington, DC 20224

We respond to many letters by telephone. Therefore, it would be helpful if you would include your daytime phone number, including the area code, in your correspondence.

Although we cannot respond individually to each comment received, we do appreciate your feedback and will consider your comments as we revise our tax products.

Ordering forms and publications. Visit www.irs.gov/formspubs to download forms and publications. Otherwise, you can go to www.irs.gov/orderforms to order current and prior-year forms and instructions. Your order should arrive within 10 business days.

Tax questions. If you have a tax question not answered by this publication, check IRS.gov and How To Get Tax Help at the end of this publication.

1.

Filing Information

Topics
This chapter discusses:

- Whether you have to file a return,
- When to file your return and pay any tax due,
- How to treat foreign currency,
- How to file electronically,
- Where to file your return,
- When you can treat your nonresident alien spouse as a resident, and
- When you may have to make estimated tax payments.

Useful Items
You may want to see:

Publication

- ❑ **3** Armed Forces' Tax Guide
- ❑ **501** Exemptions, Standard Deduction, and Filing Information
- ❑ **505** Tax Withholding and Estimated Tax
- ❑ **519** U.S. Tax Guide for Aliens
- ❑ **970** Tax Benefits for Education

Form (and Instructions)

- ❑ **1040-ES** Estimated Tax for Individuals
- ❑ **1040X** Amended U.S. Individual Income Tax Return
- ❑ **2350** Application for Extension of Time To File U.S. Income Tax Return
- ❑ **2555** Foreign Earned Income
- ❑ **2555-EZ** Foreign Earned Income Exclusion
- ❑ **4868** Application for Automatic Extension of Time To File U.S. Individual Income Tax Return
- ❑ **8822** Change of Address

See chapter 7 for information about getting these publications and forms.

Filing Requirements

If you are a U.S. citizen or resident alien, the rules for filing income, estate, and gift tax returns and for paying estimated tax are generally the same whether you are in the United States or abroad.

Your income, filing status, and age generally determine whether you must file an income tax return. Generally, you must file a return for 2015 if your gross income from worldwide sources is at least the amount shown for your filing status in the following table.

Filing Status*	Amount
Single	$10,300
65 or older	$11,850
Head of household	$13,250
65 or older	$14,800
Qualifying widow(er)	$16,600
65 or older	$17,850
Married filing jointly	$20,600
Not living with spouse at end of year	$ 4,000
One spouse 65 or older	$21,850
Both spouses 65 or older	$23,100
Married filing separately	$ 4,000

*If you are the dependent of another taxpayer, see the instructions for Form 1040 for more information on whether you must file a return.

Gross income. This includes all income you receive in the form of money, goods, property, and services that is not exempt from tax.

For purposes of determining whether you must file a return, gross income includes any income that you can exclude as foreign earned income or as a foreign housing amount.

If you are self-employed, your gross income includes the amount on Part I, line 7 of Schedule C (Form 1040), Profit or Loss From Business, or line 1 of Schedule C-EZ (Form 1040), Net Profit From Business.

Self-employed individuals. If your net earnings from self-employment are $400 or more, you must file a return even if your gross income is below the amount listed for your filing status in the table shown earlier. Net earnings from self-employment are defined in Pub. 334, Tax Guide for Small Business.

65 or older. You are considered to be age 65 on the day before your 65th birthday. For example, if your 65th birthday is on January 1, 2016, you are considered 65 for 2015.

Residents of U.S. possessions. If you are (or were) a bona fide resident of a U.S. possession, you may be required to file Form 8898, Statement for Individuals Who Begin or End Bona Fide Residence in a U.S. Possession. See the instructions for the form for more information.

When To File and Pay

If you file on a calendar year basis, the due date for filing your return is April 15 of the following year. If you file on a fiscal year basis (a year ending on the last day of any month except December), the due date is 3 months and 15 days after the close of your fiscal year. In general, the tax shown on your return should be paid by the due date of the return, without regard to any extension of time for filing the return.

When the due date for doing any act for tax purposes—filing a return, paying taxes, etc.—falls on a Saturday, Sunday, or legal holiday, the due date is delayed until the next business day.

 A tax return delivered by the U.S. mail or a designated delivery service that is postmarked or dated by the delivery service on or before the due date is considered to have been filed on or before that date. See your Form 1040 or Form 1040A instructions for a list of designated delivery services.

Direct pay option. You can pay online with a direct transfer from your bank account using Direct Pay, the Electronic Federal Tax Payment System, or by debit or credit card. You can also pay by phone using the Electronic Federal Tax Payment System or by debit or credit card. For more information, go to www.irs.gov/payments.

Foreign wire transfers. If you have a U.S. bank account, you can use:
- EFTPS (Electronic Federal Tax Payment System), or
- Federal Tax Application (same-day wire transfer).

If you do not have a U.S. bank account, ask if your financial institution has a U.S. affiliate that can help you make same-day wire transfers.

For more information, visit www.eftps.gov.

Extensions

You can get an extension of time to file your return. In some circumstances, you also can get an extension of time to file and pay any tax due.

However, if you pay the tax due after the regular due date, interest will be charged from the regular due date until the date the tax is paid.

This publication discusses four extensions: an automatic 2-month extension, an automatic 6-month extension, an additional extension for taxpayers out of the country, and an extension of time to meet tests. If you served in a combat zone or qualified hazardous duty area, see Pub. 3 for a discussion of extensions of deadlines.

Automatic 2-month extension. You are allowed an automatic 2-month extension to file your return and pay federal income tax if you are a U.S. citizen or resident alien, and on the regular due date of your return:
- You are living outside the United States and Puerto Rico and your main place of business or post of duty is outside the United States and Puerto Rico, or
- You are in military or naval service on duty outside the United States and Puerto Rico.

If you use a calendar year, the regular due date of your return is April 15. Even if you are allowed an extension, you will have to pay interest on any tax not paid by the regular due date of your return.

Married taxpayers. If you file a joint return, either you or your spouse can qualify for the automatic extension. If you and your spouse file separate returns, this automatic extension applies only to the spouse who qualifies for it.

How to get the extension. To use this automatic 2-month extension, you must attach a statement to your return explaining which of the two situations listed earlier qualified you for the extension.

Automatic 6-month extension. If you are not able to file your return by the due date, you generally can get an automatic 6-month extension of time to file (but not of time to pay). To get this automatic extension, you must file a paper Form 4868 or use IRS *e-file* (electronic filing). For more information about filing electronically, see *E-file options*, later.

The form must show your properly estimated tax liability based on the information available to you.

 You may not be eligible. You cannot use the automatic 6-month extension of time to file if:
- *You want the IRS to figure your tax, or*
- *You are under a court order to file by the regular due date.*

E-file options. You can use *e-file* to get an extension of time to file. You can either file Form 4868 electronically or you can pay part or all of your estimate of tax due using a credit or debit card.

First, complete Form 4868 to use as a worksheet. If you think you may owe tax when you file your return, use *Part II* of the form to estimate your balance due.

Then, do one of the following.

1. *E-file* **Form 4868.** You can use a tax software package with your personal computer or a tax professional to file Form 4868 electronically. You will need to provide certain information from your tax return for 2014. If you wish to make a payment by electronic funds withdrawal, see the instructions for Form 4868. If you *e-file* Form 4868, do not also send a paper Form 4868.

2. *E-file* **and pay by credit or debit card.** You can get an extension by paying part or all of your estimate of tax due by using a credit or debit card. You can do this by phone or over the Internet. If you do this, you do not file Form 4868. For more information, see the instructions for your tax return.

When to file. Generally, you must request the 6-month extension by the regular due date of your return.

Previous 2-month extension. If you cannot file your return within the automatic 2-month extension period, you generally can get an additional 4 months to file your return, for a total of 6 months. The 2-month period and the 6-month period start at the same time. You have to request the additional 4 months by the new due date allowed by the 2-month extension.

The additional 4 months of time to file (unlike the original 2-month extension) is not an extension of time to pay. You must make an accurate estimate of your tax based on the information available to you. If you find you cannot pay the full amount due with Form 4868, you can still get the extension. You will owe interest on the unpaid amount from the original due date of the return.

You also may be charged a penalty for paying the tax late unless you have reasonable cause for not paying your tax when due. Penalties for paying the tax late are assessed from the original due date of your return, unless you qualify for the automatic 2-month extension. In that situation, penalties for paying late are assessed from the extended due date of the payment (June 15 for calendar year taxpayers).

Additional extension of time for taxpayers out of the country. In addition to the 6-month extension, taxpayers who are out of the country can request a discretionary 2-month additional extension of time to file their returns (to December 15 for calendar year taxpayers).

To request this extension, you must send the Internal Revenue Service a letter explaining the reasons why you need the additional 2 months. Send the letter by the extended due date (October 15 for calendar year taxpayers) to the following address:

Department of the Treasury
Internal Revenue Service Center
Austin, TX 73301-0045

You will not receive any notification from the Internal Revenue Service unless your request is denied.

The discretionary 2-month additional extension is not available to taxpayers who have an approved extension of time to file on Form 2350, discussed next.

Extension of time to meet tests. You generally cannot get an extension of more than 6 months. However, if you are outside the United States and meet certain requirements, you may be able to get a longer extension.

You can get an extension of more than 6 months to file your tax return if you need the time to meet either the bona fide residence test or the physical presence test to qualify for either the foreign earned income exclusion or the foreign housing exclusion or deduction. The tests, the exclusions, and the deduction are explained in chapter 4.

You should request an extension if all three of the following apply.

1. You are a U.S. citizen or resident alien.

2. You expect to meet either the bona fide residence test or the physical presence test, but not until after your tax return is due.

3. Your tax home is in a foreign country (or countries) throughout your period of bona fide residence or physical presence, whichever applies.

If you are granted an extension, it generally will be to 30 days beyond the date on which you can reasonably expect to qualify for an exclusion or deduction under either the bona fide residence test or the physical presence test. However, if you have moving expenses that are for services performed in 2 years, you may be granted an extension until after the end of the second year.

How to get an extension. To obtain an extension, file Form 2350 either by giving it to a local IRS representative or other IRS employee or by mailing it to the:

Department of the Treasury
Internal Revenue Service Center
Austin, TX 73301-0045

You must file Form 2350 by the due date for filing your return. Generally, if both your tax home and your abode are outside the United States and Puerto Rico on the regular due date of your return and you file on a calendar year basis, the due date for filing your return is June 15.

What if tests are not met. If you obtain an extension and unforeseen events make it impossible for you to meet either the bona fide residence test or the physical presence test, you should file your income tax return as soon as possible because you must pay interest on any tax due after the regular due date of the return (even though an extension was granted).

You should make any request for an extension early, so that if it is denied you still can file your return on time. Otherwise, if you file late and additional tax is due, you may be subject to a penalty.

Return filed before test is met. If you file a return before you meet the bona fide residence test or the physical presence test, you must include all income from both U.S. and foreign sources and pay the tax on that income. If you later meet either of the tests, you can claim the foreign earned income exclusion, the foreign housing exclusion, or the foreign housing deduction on Form 1040X.

Foreign Currency

You must express the amounts you report on your U.S. tax return in U.S. dollars. If you receive all or part of your income, or pay some or all of your expenses, in foreign currency, you must translate the foreign currency into U.S. dollars. How you do this depends on your functional currency. Your functional currency generally is the U.S. dollar unless you are required to use the currency of a foreign country.

You must make all federal income tax determinations in your functional currency. The U.S. dollar is the functional currency for all taxpayers except some qualified business units (QBUs). A QBU is a separate and clearly identified unit of a trade or business that maintains separate books and records.

Even if you have a QBU, your functional currency is the dollar if any of the following apply.
- You conduct the business in U.S. dollars.
- The principal place of business is located in the United States.
- You choose to or are required to use the U.S. dollar as your functional currency.
- The business books and records are not kept in the currency of the economic environment in which a significant part of the business activities is conducted.

Make all income tax determinations in your functional currency. If your functional currency is the U.S. dollar, you must immediately translate into U.S. dollars all items of income, expense, etc. (including taxes), that you receive, pay, or accrue in a foreign currency and that will affect computation of your income tax. Use the exchange rate prevailing when you receive, pay, or accrue the item. You can generally get exchange rates from banks and U.S. Embassies. A taxpayer may also need to recognize foreign currency gain or loss on certain foreign currency transactions. See section 988 and the regulations thereunder.

If you have a QBU with a functional currency that is not the U.S. dollar, make all income determinations in the QBU's functional currency, and where appropriate, translate such income or loss at the appropriate exchange rate.

Blocked Income

You generally must report your foreign income in terms of U.S. dollars and, with one exception (see *Fulbright Grant,* later), you must pay taxes due on it in U.S. dollars.

If, because of restrictions in a foreign country, your income is not readily convertible into U.S. dollars or into other money or property that is readily convertible into U.S. dollars, your income is "blocked" or "deferrable" income. You can report this income in one of two ways:
- Report the income and pay your federal income tax with U.S. dollars that you have in the United States or in some other country, or
- Postpone the reporting of the income until it becomes unblocked.

If you choose to postpone the reporting of the income, you must file an information return with your tax return. For this information return, you should use another Form 1040 labeled "Report of Deferrable Foreign Income, pursuant to Rev. Rul. 74-351." You must declare on the information return that you will include the deferrable income in your taxable income for the year that it becomes unblocked. You also must state that you waive any right to claim that the deferrable income was includible in your income for any earlier year.

You must report your income on your information return using the foreign currency in which you received that income. If you have blocked income from more than one foreign country, include a separate information return for each country.

Income becomes unblocked and reportable for tax purposes when it becomes convertible, or when it is converted, into U.S. dollars or into other money or property that is convertible into U.S. currency. Also, if you use blocked income for your personal expenses or dispose of it by gift, bequest, or devise, you must treat it as unblocked and reportable.

If you have received blocked income on which you have not paid tax, you should check to see whether that income is still blocked. If it is not, you should take immediate steps to pay tax on it, file a declaration or amended declaration of estimated tax, and include the income on your tax return for the year in which the income became unblocked.

If you choose to postpone reporting blocked income and in a later tax year you wish to begin including it in gross income although it is still blocked, you must obtain the permission of the IRS to do so. To apply for permission, file Form 3115, Application for Change in Accounting Method. You also must request permission from the IRS on Form 3115 if you have not chosen to defer the reporting of blocked income in the past, but now wish to begin reporting blocked income under the deferred method. See the instructions for Form 3115 for information on changing your accounting method.

Fulbright Grant

All income must be reported in U.S. dollars. In most cases, the tax also must be paid in U.S. dollars. If, however, at least 70% of your Fulbright grant has been paid in nonconvertible foreign currency (blocked income), you can use the currency of the host country to pay the part of the U.S. tax that is based on the blocked income.

Paying U.S. tax in foreign currency. To qualify for this method of payment, you must prepare a statement that shows the following information.
- You were a Fulbright grantee and were paid in nonconvertible foreign currency.
- The total grant you received during the year and the amount you received in nonconvertible foreign currency.
- At least 70% of the grant was paid in nonconvertible foreign currency.

The statement must be certified by the U.S. educational foundation or commission paying the grant or other person having control of grant payments to you.

You should prepare at least two copies of this statement. Attach one copy to your Form 1040 and keep the other copy for identification purposes when you make a tax deposit of nonconvertible foreign currency.

Figuring actual tax. When you prepare your income tax return, you may owe tax or the entire liability may have been satisfied with your estimated tax payments. If you owe tax, figure the part due to (and payable in) the nonconvertible foreign currency by using the following formula.

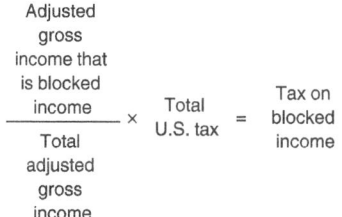

$$\frac{\text{Adjusted gross income that is blocked income}}{\text{Total adjusted gross income}} \times \text{Total U.S. tax} = \text{Tax on blocked income}$$

You must attach all of the following to the return.
- A copy of the certified statement discussed earlier.
- A detailed statement showing the allocation of tax attributable to amounts received in foreign currency and the rates of exchange used in determining your tax liability in U.S. dollars.
- The original deposit receipt for any balance of tax due that you paid in nonconvertible foreign currency.

Figuring estimated tax on nonconvertible foreign currency. If you are liable for estimated tax (discussed later), figure the amount you can pay to the IRS in nonconvertible foreign currency using the following formula.

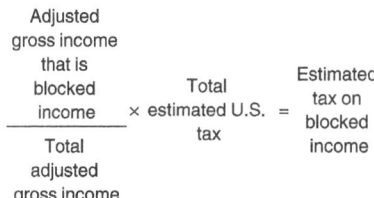

$$\frac{\text{Adjusted gross income that is blocked income}}{\text{Total adjusted gross income}} \times \text{Total estimated U.S. tax} = \text{Estimated tax on blocked income}$$

If you must pay your host country income tax on your grant, subtract any estimated foreign tax credit that applies to your grant from the estimated tax on the blocked income.

Deposit of foreign currency with disbursing officer. Once you have determined the amount of the actual tax or estimated tax that you can pay in nonconvertible foreign currency, deposit that amount with the disbursing officer of the Department of State in the foreign country in which the foundation or commission paying the grant is located.

Estimated tax installments. You can either deposit the full estimated tax amount before the first installment due date or make four equal payments before the installment due dates. See *Estimated Tax*, later.

Deposit receipt. Upon accepting the foreign currency, the disbursing officer will give you a receipt in duplicate. The original of this receipt (showing the amount of foreign currency deposited and its equivalent in U.S. dollars) should be attached to your Form 1040 or payment voucher from Form 1040-ES. Keep the copy for your records.

Does My Return Have To Be On Paper?

IRS *e-file* (electronic filing) is the fastest, easiest, and most convenient way to file your income tax return electronically.

IRS *e-file* offers accurate, safe, and fast alternatives to filing on paper. IRS computers quickly and automatically check for errors or other missing information.

Note. Returns with a foreign address can be e-filed.

How to *e-file*. There are three ways you can *e-file*.

1. Use your personal computer.

2. Use a volunteer. Many programs offering free tax help can *e-file* your return.

3. Use a tax professional. Most tax professionals can *e-file* your return.

These methods are explained in detail in the instructions for your tax return.

Where To File

If any of the following situations apply to you, do not file your return with the service center listed for your home state.
- You claim the foreign earned income exclusion.
- You claim the foreign housing exclusion or deduction.
- You live in a foreign country.

Instead, use one of the following special addresses. If you are not enclosing a check or money order, file your return with the:

Department of the Treasury
Internal Revenue Service Center
Austin, TX 73301-0215 USA

If you are enclosing a check or money order, file your return with:

Internal Revenue Service Center
P.O. Box 1303
Charlotte, NC 28201-1303 USA

If you do not know where your legal residence is and you do not have a principal place of business in the United States, you can file with the appropriate address listed above.

However, you should not file with the addresses listed above if you are a bona fide resident of the U.S. Virgin Islands, Guam, or the Commonwealth of the Northern Mariana Islands during your entire tax year.

Resident of U.S. Virgin Islands (USVI). If you are a bona fide resident of the USVI during your entire tax year, you generally are not required to file a U.S. return. However, you must file a return with the USVI.

Send your return to the:

Virgin Islands Bureau of Internal Revenue
6115 Estate Smith Bay
St. Thomas, Virgin Islands 00802

Non-USVI resident with USVI income. If you are a U.S. citizen or resident alien and you have income from sources in the USVI or income effectively connected with the conduct of a trade or business in the USVI, and you are not a bona fide resident of the USVI during your entire tax year, you must file identical tax returns with the United States and the USVI. File the original return with the United States and file a signed copy of the U.S. return (including all attachments, forms, and schedules) with the Virgin Islands Bureau of Internal Revenue.

You must complete Form 8689, Allocation of Individual Income Tax to the U.S. Virgin Islands, and attach a copy to both your U.S. return and your USVI return. You should file your U.S. return with the address listed under *Where To File.*

See Pub. 570, Tax Guide for Individuals With Income From U.S. Possessions, for information about filing Virgin Islands returns.

Resident of Guam. If you are a bona fide resident of Guam during your entire tax year, you should file a return with Guam.

Send your return to the:

Department of Revenue and Taxation
Government of Guam
P.O. Box 23607
GMF, GU 96921

However, if you have income from sources within Guam and you are a U.S. citizen or resident alien, but not a bona fide resident of Guam during your entire tax year, you should file a return with the United States. Send your return to the address listed under *Where To File.*

See Pub. 570 for information about filing Guam returns.

Resident of the Commonwealth of the Northern Mariana Islands. If you are a bona fide resident of the Commonwealth of the Northern Mariana Islands (CNMI) during your entire tax year, you should file a return with the Northern Mariana Islands.

Send your return to the:

Division of Revenue and Taxation
Commonwealth of the Northern Mariana Islands
P.O. Box 5234, CHRB
Saipan, MP 96950

However, if you have income from sources within the CNMI and you are a U.S. citizen or resident alien, but not a bona fide resident of the CNMI during the entire tax year, you should file a return with the United States. Send your return to the address listed under *Where To File.*

See Pub. 570 for information about filing Northern Mariana Islands returns.

Nonresident Alien Spouse Treated as a Resident

If, at the end of your tax year, you are married and one spouse is a U.S. citizen or a resident alien and the other is a nonresident alien, you can choose to treat the nonresident as a U.S. resident. This includes situations in which one of you is a nonresident alien at the beginning of the tax year and a resident alien at the end of the year and the other is a nonresident alien at the end of the year.

If you make this choice, the following two rules apply.
- You and your spouse are treated, for income tax purposes, as residents for all tax years that the choice is in effect.
- You must file a joint income tax return for the year you make the choice.

This means that neither of you can claim under any tax treaty not to be a U.S. resident for a tax year for which the choice is in effect.

You can file joint or separate returns in years after the year in which you make the choice.

Example 1. Pat Smith, a U.S. citizen, is married to Norman, a nonresident alien. Pat and Norman make the choice to treat Norman as a resident alien by attaching a statement to their joint return. Pat and Norman must report their worldwide income for the year they make the choice and for all later years unless the choice is ended or suspended. Although Pat and Norman must file a joint return for the year they make the choice, they can file either joint or separate returns for later years.

Example 2. When Bob and Sharon Williams got married, both were nonresident aliens. In June of last year, Bob became a resident alien and remained a resident for the rest of the year. Bob and Sharon both choose to be treated as resident aliens by attaching a statement to their joint return for last year. Bob and Sharon must report their worldwide income for last year and all later years unless the choice is ended or suspended. Bob and Sharon must file a joint return for last year, but they can file either joint or separate returns for later years.

 If you do not choose to treat your non-resident alien spouse as a U.S. resident, you may be able to use head of household filing status. To use this status, you must pay more than half the cost of maintaining a household for certain dependents or relatives other than your nonresident alien spouse. For more information, see Pub. 501.

Social Security Number (SSN)

If you choose to treat your nonresident alien spouse as a U.S. resident, your spouse must have either an SSN or an individual taxpayer identification number (ITIN).

To get an SSN for a nonresident alien spouse, apply at an office of the U.S. Social Security Administration (SSA) or U.S. consulate. You must complete Form SS-5, Application for a Social Security Card, available at www.socialsecurity.gov or by calling 1-800-772-1213. You must also provide original or certified copies of documents to verify that spouse's age, identity, and citizenship.

If the nonresident alien spouse is not eligible to get an SSN, he or she can file Form W-7, Application for IRS Individual Taxpayer Identification Number, with the IRS to apply for an ITIN.

How To Make the Choice

Attach a statement, signed by both spouses, to your joint return for the first tax year for which the choice applies. It should contain the following:

- A declaration that one spouse was a nonresident alien and the other spouse a U.S. citizen or resident alien on the last day of your tax year and that you choose to be treated as U.S. residents for the entire tax year, and
- The name, address, and social security number (or individual taxpayer identification number) of each spouse. (If one spouse died, include the name and address of the person making the choice for the deceased spouse.)

You generally make this choice when you file your joint return. However, you also can make the choice by filing a joint amended return on Form 1040X. Attach Form 1040, 1040A, or 1040EZ and print "Amended" across the top of the amended return. If you make the choice with an amended return, you and your spouse also must amend any returns that you may have filed after the year for which you made the choice.

You generally must file the amended joint return within 3 years from the date you filed your original U.S. income tax return or 2 years from the date you paid your income tax for that year, whichever is later.

Suspending the Choice

The choice to be treated as a resident alien does not apply to any later tax year if neither of you is a U.S. citizen or resident alien at any time during the later tax year.

Example. Dick Brown was a resident alien on December 31, 2012, and married to Judy, a nonresident alien. They chose to treat Judy as a resident alien and filed joint income tax returns for 2012 and 2013. On January 10, 2014, Dick became a nonresident alien. Judy had remained a nonresident alien. Because Dick was a resident alien during part of 2014, Dick and Judy can file joint or separate returns for that year. Neither Dick nor Judy was a resident alien at any time during 2015 and their choice is suspended for that year. For 2015, both are treated as nonresident aliens. If Dick becomes a resident alien again in 2016, their choice is no longer suspended and both are treated as resident aliens.

Ending the Choice

Once made, the choice to be treated as a resident applies to all later years unless suspended (as explained earlier) or ended in one of the ways shown in Table 1-1.

If the choice is ended for any of the reasons listed in Table 1-1, neither spouse can make a choice in any later tax year.

Estimated Tax

The requirements for determining who must pay estimated tax are the same for a U.S. citizen or resident abroad as for a taxpayer in the United States. For current instructions on making estimated tax payments, see Form 1040-ES.

If you had a tax liability for 2015, you may have to pay estimated tax for 2016. Generally, you must make estimated tax payments for 2016 if you expect to owe at least $1,000 in tax

Table 1–1. Ending the Choice To Treat Nonresident Alien Spouse as a Resident

Revocation	**Either spouse can revoke the choice for any tax year.**
	• The revocation must be made by the due date for filing the tax return for that tax year.
	• The spouse who revokes the choice must attach a signed statement declaring that the choice is being revoked. The statement revoking the choice must include the following:
	• The name, address, and social security number (or taxpayer identification number) of each spouse.
	• The name and address of any person who is revoking the choice for a deceased spouse.
	• A list of any states, foreign countries, and possessions that have community property laws in which either spouse is domiciled or where real property is located from which either spouse receives income.
	• If the spouse revoking the choice does not have to file a return and does not file a claim for refund, send the statement to the Internal Revenue Service Center where the last joint return was filed.
Death	**The death of either spouse ends the choice, beginning with the first tax year following the year in which the spouse died.**
	• If the surviving spouse is a U.S. citizen or resident alien and is entitled to the joint tax rates as a surviving spouse, the choice will not end until the close of the last year for which these joint rates may be used.
	• If both spouses die in the same tax year, the choice ends on the first day after the close of the tax year in which the spouses died.
Divorce or Legal separation	**A divorce or legal separation ends the choice as of the beginning of the tax year in which the legal separation occurs.**
Inadequate records	**The Internal Revenue Service can end the choice for any tax year that either spouse has failed to keep adequate books, records, and other information necessary to determine the correct income tax liability, or to provide adequate access to those records.**

for 2016 after subtracting your withholding and credits and you expect your withholding and credits to be less than the smaller of:

1. 90% of the tax to be shown on your 2016 tax return, or

2. 100% of the tax shown on your 2015 tax return. (The return must cover all 12 months.)

If less than two-thirds of your gross income for 2015 and 2016 is from farming or fishing and your adjusted gross income for 2015 is more than $150,000 ($75,000 if you are married and file separately), substitute 110% for 100% in (2). See Pub. 505 for more information.

The first installment of estimated tax is due on April 18, 2016.

Foreign earned income exclusion. When figuring your estimated gross income, subtract amounts you expect to exclude under the foreign earned income exclusion and the foreign housing exclusion. In addition, you can reduce your income by your estimated foreign housing deduction. However, you must estimate tax on your nonexcluded income using the tax rates that will apply had you not excluded the income. If the actual amount of the exclusion or deduction is less than you estimate, you may have to pay a penalty for underpayment of estimated tax.

For more information about figuring your estimated tax, see Pub. 505.

Other Forms You May Have To File

FinCEN Form 114. You must file Form 114, Report of Foreign Bank and Financial Accounts (FBAR), if you had any financial interest in, or signature or other authority over a bank, securities, or other financial account in a foreign country. You do not need to file the report if the assets are with a U.S. military banking facility operated by a financial institution or if the combined assets in the account(s) are $10,000 or less during the entire year.

Form 114 is filed electronically with the Financial Crimes Enforcement Network (FinCEN). See the filing instructions at *www.bsaefiling.fincen.treas.gov/main.html*.

FinCEN Form 105. You must file Form 105, Report of International Transportation of Currency or Monetary Instruments, if you physically transport, mail, ship, or cause to be physically transported, mailed, or shipped into or out of the United States, currency or other monetary instruments totaling more than $10,000 at one time. Certain recipients of currency or monetary instruments also must file Form 105.

More information about the filing of Form 105 can be found in the instructions on the back of the form available at *www.fincen.gov/forms/bsa_forms/*.

Form 8938. You must file Form 8938 to report the ownership of specified foreign financial assets if the total value of those assets exceeds an applicable threshold amount (the "reporting threshold"). The reporting threshold varies depending on whether you live in the United States, are married, or file a joint income tax return with your spouse. Specified foreign financial assets include any financial account maintained by a foreign financial institution and, to the extent held for investment, any stock, securities, or any other interest in a foreign entity and any financial instrument or contract with an issuer or counterparty that is not a U.S. person.

You may have to pay penalties if you are required to file Form 8938 and fail to do so, or if you have an understatement of tax due to any transaction involving an undisclosed foreign financial asset.

More information about the filing of Form 8938 can be found in the separate instructions for Form 8938.

2.

Withholding Tax

Topics
This chapter discusses:

- Withholding income tax from the pay of U.S. citizens,
- Withholding tax at a flat rate, and
- Social security and Medicare taxes.

Useful Items
You may want to see:

Publication

❑ **505** Tax Withholding and Estimated Tax

Form (and Instructions)

❑ **673** Statement For Claiming Exemption From Withholding on Foreign Earned Income Eligible for the Exclusion Provided by Section 911

❑ **W-4** Employee's Withholding Allowance Certificate

❑ **W-9** Request for Taxpayer Identification Number and Certification

See chapter 7 for information about getting this publication and these forms.

Income Tax Withholding

U.S. employers generally must withhold U.S. income tax from the pay of U.S. citizens working abroad unless the employer is required by foreign law to withhold foreign income tax.

Foreign earned income exclusion. Your employer does not have to withhold U.S. income taxes from wages you earn abroad if it is reasonable to believe that you will exclude them from income under the foreign earned income exclusion or the foreign housing exclusion.

Your employer should withhold taxes from any wages you earn for working in the United States.

Statement. You can give a statement to your employer indicating that you expect to qualify for the foreign earned income exclusion under either the bona fide residence test or the physical presence test and indicating your estimated housing cost exclusion.

Form 673 is an acceptable statement. You can use Form 673 only if you are a U.S. citizen. You do not have to use the form. You can prepare your own statement. See a copy of Form 673, later.

Generally, your employer can stop the withholding once you submit the statement that includes a declaration that the statement is made under penalties of perjury. However, if your employer has reason to believe that you will not qualify for either the foreign earned income or the foreign housing exclusion, your employer must continue to withhold.

In determining whether your foreign earned income is more than the limit on either the foreign earned income exclusion or the foreign housing exclusion, if your employer has any information about pay you received from any other source outside the United States, your employer must take that information into account.

Foreign tax credit. If you plan to take a foreign tax credit, you may be eligible for additional withholding allowances on Form W-4. You can take these additional withholding allowances only for foreign tax credits attributable to taxable salary or wage income.

Withholding from pension payments. U.S. payers of benefits from employer-deferred compensation plans, individual retirement plans, and commercial annuities generally must withhold income tax from payments delivered outside of the United States. You can choose exemption from withholding if you:

- Provide the payer of the benefits with a residence address in the United States or a U.S. possession, or
- Certify to the payer that you are not a U.S. citizen or resident alien or someone who left the United States to avoid tax.

Check your withholding. Before you report U.S. income tax withholding on your tax return, you should carefully review all information documents, such as Form W-2, Wage and Tax Statement, and the Form 1099 information returns. Compare other records, such as final pay records or bank statements, with Form W-2 or Form 1099 to verify the withholding on these forms. Check your U.S. income tax withholding even if you pay someone else to prepare your tax return. You may be assessed penalties and interest if you claim more than your correct amount of withholding allowances.

Form 673
(Rev. December 2007)
Department of the Treasury
Internal Revenue Service

Statement for Claiming Exemption From Withholding on Foreign Earned Income Eligible for the Exclusion(s) Provided by Section 911

OMB No. 1545-0074

The following statement, when completed and furnished by a citizen of the United States to his or her employer, permits the employer to exclude from income tax withholding all or a part of the wages paid for services performed outside the United States.

Name *(please print or type)* | **Social security number**

| **Part I** | **Qualification Information for Foreign Earned Income Exclusion** |

I expect to qualify for the foreign earned income exclusion under either the bona fide residence or physical presence test for calendar year _____ or other tax year beginning _____ and ending _____ .

Please check applicable box:

☐ **Bona Fide Residence Test**

I am a citizen of the United States. I have been a bona fide resident of and my tax home has been located in _____ (foreign country or countries) for an uninterrupted period which includes an entire tax year that began on _____, 20 _____ .
(date)

I expect to remain a bona fide resident and retain my tax home in a foreign country (or countries) until the end of the tax year for which this statement is made. Or, if not that period, from the date of this statement until _____, 20 _____ .
(date within tax year)

I have not submitted a statement to the authorities of any foreign country named above that I am not a resident of that country. Or, if I made such a statement, the authorities of that country thereafter made a determination to the effect that I am a resident of that country.

Based on the facts in my case, I have good reason to believe that for this period of foreign residence I will satisfy the tax home and the bona fide foreign resident requirements prescribed by section 911(d)(1)(A) of the Internal Revenue Code and qualify for the exclusion Code section 911(a) allows.

☐ **Physical Presence Test**

I am a citizen of the United States. Except for occasional absences that will not disqualify me for the benefit of section 911(a) of the Internal Revenue Code, I expect to be present in and maintain my tax home in _____ (foreign country or countries) for a 12-month period that includes the entire tax year _____ . Or, if not the entire year, for the part of the tax year beginning on _____, 20 _____ , and ending on _____, 20 _____ .

Based on the facts in my case, I have good reason to believe that for this period of presence in a foreign country or countries, I will satisfy the tax home and the 330 full-day requirements within a 12-month period under section 911(d)(1)(B).

Part II	**Estimated Housing Cost Amount for Foreign Housing Exclusion** (see instructions)		
1	Rent	1	
2	Utilities (other than telephone charges)	2	
3	Real and personal property insurance	3	
4	Occupancy tax not deductible under section 164	4	
5	Nonrefundable fees paid for securing a leasehold	5	
6	Household repairs	6	
7	**Estimated qualified housing expenses.** Add lines 1 through 6	7	
8	Estimated base housing amount for qualifying period	8	
9	Subtract line 8 from line 7. This is your estimated housing cost amount	9	

| **Part III** | **Certification** |

Under penalties of perjury, I declare that I have examined the information on this form and to the best of my knowledge and belief it is true, correct, and complete. I further certify under penalties of perjury that:

• The estimated housing cost amount entered in Part II, plus the amount reported on any other statements outstanding with other employers, is not more than my total estimated housing cost amount.

• If I become disqualified for the exclusions, I will immediately notify my employer and advise what part, if any, of the period for which I am qualified.

I understand that any exemption from income tax withholding permitted by reason of furnishing this statement is not a determination by the Internal Revenue Service that any amount paid to me for any services performed during the tax year is excludable from gross income under the provisions of Code section 911(a).

Your Signature | Date

For Paperwork Reduction Act Notice, see back of form. | Cat. No. 10183Y | Form **673** (Rev. 12-2007)

30% Flat Rate Withholding

Generally, U.S. payers of income other than wages, such as dividends and royalties, are required to withhold tax at a flat 30% (or lower treaty) rate on nonwage income paid to nonresident aliens. If you are a U.S. citizen or resident alien and this tax is withheld in error from payments to you because you have a foreign address, you should notify the payer of the income to stop the withholding. Use Form W-9 to notify the payer.

You can claim the tax withheld in error as a withholding credit on your tax return if the amount is not adjusted by the payer.

Social security benefits paid to residents. If you are a lawful permanent resident (green card holder) and a flat 30% tax was withheld in error on your social security benefits, the tax is refundable by the Social Security Administration (SSA) or the IRS. The SSA will refund the tax withheld if the refund can be processed during the same calendar year in which the tax was withheld. If the SSA cannot refund the tax withheld, you must file a Form 1040 or 1040A with the Internal Revenue Service Center at the address listed under *Where To File* to determine if you are entitled to a refund. The following information must be submitted with your Form 1040 or Form 1040A.

- A copy of Form SSA-1042S, Social Security Benefit Statement.
- A copy of your "green card."
- A signed declaration that includes the following statements.

"I am a U.S. lawful permanent resident and my green card has been neither revoked nor administratively or judicially determined to have been abandoned. I am filing a U.S. income tax return for the taxable year as a resident alien reporting all of my worldwide income. I have not claimed benefits for the taxable year under an income tax treaty as a nonresident alien."

Social Security and Medicare Taxes

Social security and Medicare taxes may apply to wages paid to an employee regardless of where the services are performed.

General Information

In general, U.S. social security and Medicare taxes do not apply to wages for services you perform as an employee outside the United States unless one of the following exceptions applies.

1. You perform the services on or in connection with an American vessel or aircraft (defined later) and either:

    a. You entered into your employment contract within the United States, or

    b. The vessel or aircraft touches at a U.S. port while you are employed on it.

2. You are working in one of the countries with which the United States has entered into a bilateral social security agreement (discussed later).

3. You are working for an American employer (defined later).

4. You are working for a foreign affiliate (defined later) of an American employer under a voluntary agreement entered into between the American employer and the U.S. Treasury Department.

American vessel or aircraft. An American vessel is any vessel documented or numbered under the laws of the United States and any other vessel whose crew is employed solely by one or more U.S. citizens, residents, or corporations. An American aircraft is an aircraft registered under the laws of the United States.

American employer. An American employer includes any of the following.
- The U.S. Government or any of its instrumentalities.
- An individual who is a resident of the United States.
- A partnership of which at least two-thirds of the partners are U.S. residents.
- A trust of which all the trustees are U.S. residents.
- A corporation organized under the laws of the United States, any U.S. state, or the District of Columbia, Puerto Rico, the U.S. Virgin Islands, Guam, or American Samoa.

An American employer also includes any foreign person with an employee who is performing services in connection with a contract between the U.S. government (or any instrumentality thereof) and a member of a domestically controlled group of entities which includes such foreign person.

Foreign affiliate. A foreign affiliate of an American employer is any foreign entity in which the American employer has at least a 10% interest, directly or through one or more entities. For a corporation, the 10% interest must be in its voting stock. For any other entity, the 10% interest must be in its profits.

Form 2032 is used by American employers to extend social security coverage to U.S. citizens and resident aliens working abroad for foreign affiliates of American employers. Once you enter into an agreement, coverage cannot be terminated.

Excludable meals and lodging. Social security tax does not apply to the value of meals and lodging provided to you for the convenience of your employer if it is reasonable to believe that you will be able to exclude the value from your income.

Bilateral Social Security (Totalization) Agreements

The United States has entered into agreements with some foreign countries to coordinate social security coverage and taxation of workers who are employed in those countries. These agreements are commonly referred to as totalization agreements. Under these agreements, dual coverage and dual contributions (taxes) for the same work are eliminated. The agreements generally make sure that you pay social security taxes to only one country.

Generally, under these agreements, you will only be subject to social security taxes in the country where you are working. However, if you are temporarily sent to work in a foreign country and your pay would otherwise be subject to social security taxes in both the United States and that country, you generally can remain covered only by U.S. social security.

You can get more information on specific agreements at *www.socialsecurity.gov/international/agreement_descriptions.html*.

Or, you can write to:

Social Security Administration
Office of International Programs
P.O. Box 17741
Baltimore, MD 21235-7741

Covered by U.S. only. If your pay in a foreign country is subject only to U.S. social security tax and is exempt from foreign social security tax, your employer should get a certificate of coverage from the Office of International Programs. Employers can request a certificate of coverage online at *www.socialsecurity.gov/coc*.

Covered by foreign country only. If you are permanently working in a foreign country with which the United States has a social security agreement and, under the agreement, your pay is exempt from U.S. social security tax, you or your employer should get a statement from the authorized official or agency of the foreign country verifying that your pay is subject to social security coverage in that country.

If the authorities of the foreign country will not issue such a statement, either you or your employer should get a statement from the U.S. Social Security Administration, Office of International Programs, at the website and mailing addresses listed earlier. The statement should indicate that your wages are not covered by the U.S. social security system.

This statement should be kept by your employer because it establishes that your pay is exempt from U.S. social security tax.

Only wages paid on or after the effective date of the totalization agreement can be exempt from U.S. social security tax.

3.

Self-Employment Tax

Topics
This chapter discusses:

- Who must pay self-employment tax, and
- Who is exempt from self-employment tax.

Useful Items
You may want to see:

Publication

❏ **334** Tax Guide for Small Business

❏ **517** Social Security and Other Information for Members of the Clergy and Religious Workers

Form (and Instructions)

❏ **Form 1040-PR** Planilla para la Declaración de la Contribución Federal sobre el Trabajo por Cuenta Propia

❏ **Form 1040-SS** U.S. Self-Employment Tax Return

❏ **Form 4361** Application for Exemption From Self-Employment Tax for Use by Ministers, Members of Religious Orders and Christian Science Practitioners

❏ **Schedule SE (Form 1040)** Self-Employment Tax

See chapter 7 for information about getting these publications and forms.

Who Must Pay Self-Employment Tax?

If you are a self-employed U.S. citizen or resident, the rules for paying self-employment tax are generally the same whether you are living in the United States or abroad.

The self-employment tax is a social security and Medicare tax on net earnings from self-employment. You must pay self-employment tax if your net earnings from self-employment are at least $400.

For 2015, the maximum amount of net earnings from self-employment that is subject to the social security portion of the tax is $118,500. All net earnings are subject to the Medicare portion of the tax.

Employed by a U.S. Church

If you were employed by a U.S. church or a qualified church-controlled organization that chose exemption from social security and Medicare taxes and you received wages of $108.28 or more from the organization, the amounts paid to you are subject to self-employment tax. However, you can choose to be exempt from social security and Medicare taxes if you are a member of a recognized religious sect. See Pub. 517 for more information about church employees and self-employment tax.

Effect of Exclusion

You must take all of your self-employment income into account in figuring your net earnings from self-employment, even income that is exempt from income tax because of the foreign earned income exclusion.

Example. You are in business abroad as a consultant and qualify for the foreign earned income exclusion. Your foreign earned income is $95,000, your business deductions total $27,000, and your net profit is $68,000. You must pay self-employment tax on all of your net profit, including the amount you can exclude from income.

Members of the Clergy

If you are a member of the clergy, you are treated as self-employed for self-employment tax purposes. Your U.S. self-employment tax is based upon net earnings from self-employment figured without regard to the foreign earned income exclusion or the foreign housing exclusion.

You can receive exemption from coverage for your ministerial duties if you conscientiously oppose public insurance due to religious reasons or if you oppose it due to the religious principles of your denomination. You must file Form 4361 to apply for this exemption.

This subject is discussed in further detail in Pub. 517.

Income From U.S. Possessions

If you are a U.S. citizen or resident alien and you own and operate a business in Puerto Rico, Guam, the Commonwealth of the Northern Mariana Islands, American Samoa, or the U.S. Virgin Islands, you must pay tax on your net earnings from self-employment (if they are $400 or more) from those sources. You must pay the self-employment tax whether or not the income is exempt from U.S. income taxes (or whether or not you otherwise must file a U.S. income tax return). Unless your situation is described below, attach Schedule SE (Form 1040) to your U.S. income tax return.

If you do not have to file Form 1040 with the United States and you are a resident of any of the U.S. possessions listed in the preceding paragraph, figure your self-employment tax on Form 1040-SS. Residents of Puerto Rico may file the Spanish-language Formulario 1040-PR.

If you are not enclosing a check or money order, file your return with the:

Department of the Treasury
Internal Revenue Service Center
Austin, TX 73301-0215

If you are enclosing a check or money order, file your return with the:

Department of the Treasury
P.O. Box 1303
Charlotte, NC 28201-1303

Exemption From Social Security and Medicare Taxes

The United States may reach agreements with foreign countries to eliminate dual coverage and dual contributions (taxes) to social security systems for the same work. See *Bilateral Social Security (Totalization) Agreements* in chapter 2 under *Social Security and Medicare Taxes*. As a general rule, self-employed persons who are subject to dual taxation will only be covered by the social security system of the country where they reside. For more information on how a specific agreement affects self-employed persons, see *Bilateral Social Security (Totalization) Agreements* in chapter 2.

If your self-employment earnings should be exempt from foreign social security tax and subject only to U.S. self-employment tax, you should request a certificate of coverage from the U.S. Social Security Administration, Office of International Programs. The certificate will establish your exemption from the foreign social security tax.

You can request a certificate of coverage online at *www.socialsecurity.gov/coc*.

4.

Foreign Earned Income and Housing: Exclusion – Deduction

Topics
This chapter discusses:

- Who qualifies for the foreign earned income exclusion, the foreign housing exclusion, and the foreign housing deduction,

- The requirements that must be met to claim either exclusion or the deduction,
- How to figure the foreign earned income exclusion, and
- How to figure the foreign housing exclusion and the foreign housing deduction.

Useful Items

You may want to see:

Publication

❏ **519** U.S. Tax Guide for Aliens

❏ **570** Tax Guide for Individuals With Income from U.S. Possessions

❏ **596** Earned Income Credit (EIC)

Form (and Instructions)

❏ **1040X** Amended U.S. Individual Income Tax Return

❏ **2555** Foreign Earned Income

❏ **2555-EZ** Foreign Earned Income Exclusion

See chapter 7 for information about getting these publications and forms.

Who Qualifies for the Exclusions and the Deduction?

If you meet certain requirements, you may qualify for the foreign earned income and foreign housing exclusions and the foreign housing deduction.

If you are a U.S. citizen or a resident alien of the United States and you live abroad, you are taxed on your worldwide income. However, you may qualify to exclude from income up to $100,800 of your foreign earnings. In addition, you can exclude or deduct certain foreign housing amounts. See *Foreign Earned Income Exclusion* and *Foreign Housing Exclusion and Deduction*, later.

You also may be entitled to exclude from income the value of meals and lodging provided to you by your employer. See *Exclusion of Meals and Lodging*, later.

Requirements

To claim the foreign earned income exclusion, the foreign housing exclusion, or the foreign housing deduction, you must meet all three of the following requirements.

1. Your tax home must be in a foreign country.

2. You must have foreign earned income.

3. You must be one of the following.

    a. A U.S. citizen who is a bona fide resident of a foreign country or countries for an uninterrupted period that includes an entire tax year.

    b. A U.S. resident alien who is a citizen or national of a country with which the United States has an income tax treaty in effect and who is a bona fide resident of a foreign country or countries for an uninterrupted period that includes an entire tax year.

    c. A U.S. citizen or a U.S. resident alien who is physically present in a foreign country or countries for at least 330 full days during any period of 12 consecutive months.

See Pub. 519 to find out if you are a U.S. resident alien for tax purposes and whether you keep that alien status when you temporarily work abroad.

If you are a nonresident alien married to a U.S. citizen or resident alien, and both you and your spouse choose to treat you as a resident alien, you are a resident alien for tax purposes. For information on making the choice, see the discussion in chapter 1 under *Nonresident Alien Spouse Treated as a Resident*.

Waiver of minimum time requirements. The minimum time requirements for bona fide residence and physical presence can be waived if you must leave a foreign country because of war, civil unrest, or similar adverse conditions in that country. This is fully explained under *Waiver of Time Requirements*, later.

See Figure 4-A and information in this chapter to determine if you are eligible to claim either exclusion or the deduction.

Tax Home in Foreign Country

To qualify for the foreign earned income exclusion, the foreign housing exclusion, or the foreign housing deduction, your tax home must be in a foreign country throughout your period of bona fide residence or physical presence abroad. Bona fide residence and physical presence are explained later.

Tax Home

Your tax home is the general area of your main place of business, employment, or post of duty, regardless of where you maintain your family home. Your tax home is the place where you are permanently or indefinitely engaged to work as an employee or self-employed individual. Having a "tax home" in a given location does not necessarily mean that the given location is your residence or domicile for tax purposes.

If you do not have a regular or main place of business because of the nature of your work, your tax home may be the place where you regularly live. If you have neither a regular or main place of business nor a place where you regularly live, you are considered an itinerant and your tax home is wherever you work.

You are not considered to have a tax home in a foreign country for any period in which your abode is in the United States. However, your abode is not necessarily in the United States while you are temporarily in the United States.

Your abode is also not necessarily in the United States merely because you maintain a dwelling in the United States, whether or not your spouse or dependents use the dwelling.

"Abode" has been variously defined as one's home, habitation, residence, domicile, or place of dwelling. It does not mean your principal place of business. "Abode" has a domestic rather than a vocational meaning and does not mean the same as "tax home." The location of your abode often will depend on where you maintain your economic, family, and personal ties.

Example 1. You are employed on an offshore oil rig in the territorial waters of a foreign country and work a 28-day on/28-day off schedule. You return to your family residence in the United States during your off periods. You are considered to have an abode in the United States and do not satisfy the tax home test in the foreign country. You cannot claim either of the exclusions or the housing deduction.

Example 2. For several years, you were a marketing executive with a producer of machine tools in Toledo, Ohio. In November of last year, your employer transferred you to London, England, for a minimum of 18 months to set up a sales operation for Europe. Before you left, you distributed business cards showing your business and home addresses in London. You kept ownership of your home in Toledo but rented it to another family. You placed your car in storage. In November of last year, you moved your spouse, children, furniture, and family pets to a home your employer rented for you in London.

Shortly after moving, you leased a car and you and your spouse got British driving licenses. Your entire family got library cards for the local public library. You and your spouse opened bank accounts with a London bank and secured consumer credit. You joined a local business league and both you and your spouse became active in the neighborhood civic association and worked with a local charity. Your abode is in London for the time you live there. You satisfy the tax home test in the foreign country.

Temporary or Indefinite Assignment

The location of your tax home often depends on whether your assignment is temporary or indefinite. If you are temporarily absent from your tax home in the United States on business, you may be able to deduct your away-from-home expenses (for travel, meals, and lodging), but you would not qualify for the foreign earned income exclusion. If your new work assignment is for an indefinite period, your new place of employment becomes your tax home and you would not be able to deduct any of the related expenses that you have in the general area of this new work assignment. If your new tax home is in a foreign country and you meet the other requirements, your earnings may qualify for the foreign earned income exclusion.

If you expect your employment away from home in a single location to last, and it does

Figure 4–A. Can I Claim Either Exclusion or the Deduction?

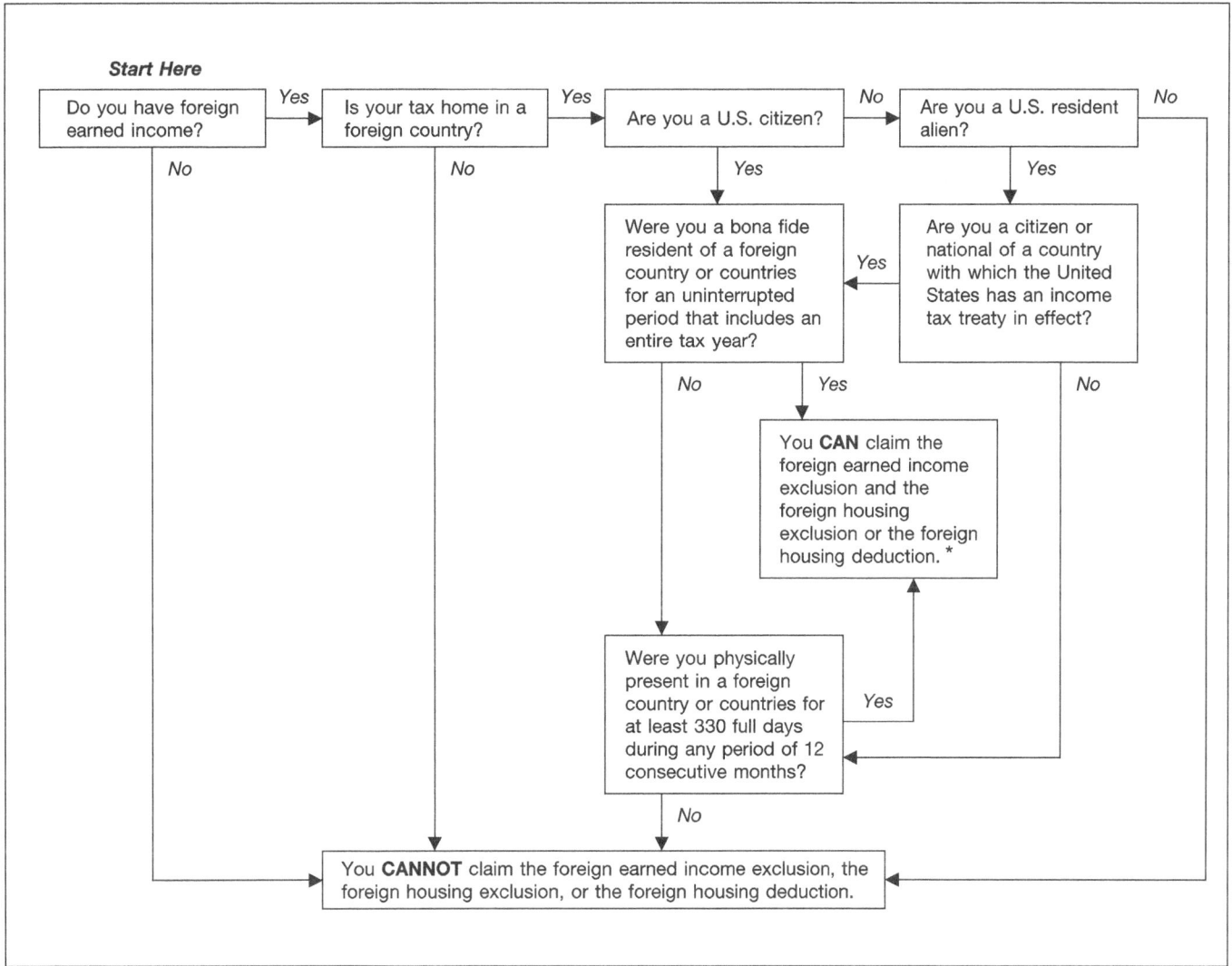

* Foreign housing exclusion applies only to employees. Foreign housing deduction applies only to the self-employed.

last, for 1 year or less, it is temporary unless facts and circumstances indicate otherwise.

If you expect it to last for more than 1 year, it is indefinite.

If you expect it to last for 1 year or less, but at some later date you expect it to last longer than 1 year, it is temporary (in the absence of facts and circumstances indicating otherwise) until your expectation changes. Once your expectation changes, it is indefinite.

Foreign Country

To meet the bona fide residence test or the physical presence test, you must live in or be present in a foreign country. A foreign country includes any territory under the sovereignty of a government other than that of the United States.

The term "foreign country" includes the country's airspace and territorial waters, but not international waters and the airspace above them. It also includes the seabed and subsoil of those submarine areas adjacent to the country's

territorial waters over which it has exclusive rights under international law to explore and exploit the natural resources.

The term "foreign country" does not include Antarctica or U.S. possessions such as Puerto Rico, Guam, the Commonwealth of the Northern Mariana Islands, the U.S. Virgin Islands, and Johnston Island. For purposes of the foreign earned income exclusion, the foreign housing exclusion, and the foreign housing deduction, the terms "foreign," "abroad," and "overseas" refer to areas outside the United States and those areas listed or described in the previous sentence.

American Samoa, Guam, and the Commonwealth of the Northern Mariana Islands

Residence or presence in a U.S. possession does not qualify you for the foreign earned income exclusion. You may, however, qualify for an exclusion of your possession income on your U.S. return.

American Samoa. There is a possession exclusion available to individuals who are bona fide residents of American Samoa for the entire tax year. Gross income from sources within American Samoa may be eligible for this exclusion. Income that is effectively connected with the conduct of a trade or business within American Samoa also may be eligible for this exclusion. Use Form 4563 to figure the exclusion.

Guam and the Commonwealth of the Northern Mariana Islands. An exclusion will be available to residents of Guam and the Commonwealth of the Northern Mariana Islands if, and when, new implementation agreements take effect between the United States and those possessions.

For more information, see Pub. 570.

Puerto Rico and U.S. Virgin Islands

Residents of Puerto Rico and the U.S. Virgin Islands cannot claim the foreign earned income exclusion or the foreign housing exclusion.

Puerto Rico. Generally, if you are a U.S. citizen who is a bona fide resident of Puerto Rico for the entire tax year, you are not subject to U.S. tax on income from Puerto Rican sources. This does not include amounts paid for services performed as an employee of the United States. However, you are subject to U.S. tax on your income from sources outside Puerto Rico. In figuring your U.S. tax, you cannot deduct expenses allocable to income not subject to tax.

Bona Fide Residence Test

You meet the bona fide residence test if you are a bona fide resident of a foreign country or countries for an uninterrupted period that includes an entire tax year. You can use the bona fide residence test to qualify for the exclusions and the deduction only if you are either:

● A U.S. citizen, or

● A U.S. resident alien who is a citizen or national of a country with which the United States has an income tax treaty in effect.

You do not automatically acquire bona fide resident status merely by living in a foreign country or countries for 1 year. If you go to a foreign country to work on a particular job for a specified period of time, you ordinarily will not be regarded as a bona fide resident of that country even though you work there for 1 tax year or longer. The length of your stay and the nature of your job are only two of the factors to be considered in determining whether you meet the bona fide residence test.

Bona fide residence. To meet the bona fide residence test, you must have established a bona fide residence in a foreign country.

Your bona fide residence is not necessarily the same as your domicile. Your domicile is your permanent home, the place to which you always return or intend to return.

Example. You could have your domicile in Cleveland, Ohio, and a bona fide residence in Edinburgh, Scotland, if you intend to return eventually to Cleveland.

The fact that you go to Scotland does not automatically make Scotland your bona fide residence. If you go there as a tourist, or on a short business trip, and return to the United States, you have not established bona fide residence in Scotland. But if you go to Scotland to work for an indefinite or extended period and you set up permanent quarters there for yourself and your family, you probably have established a bona fide residence in a foreign country, even though you intend to return eventually to the United States.

You are clearly not a resident of Scotland in the first instance. However, in the second, you are a resident because your stay in Scotland appears to be permanent. If your residency is not as clearly defined as either of these illustrations, it may be more difficult to decide whether you have established a bona fide residence.

Determination. Questions of bona fide residence are determined according to each individual case, taking into account factors such as your intention, the purpose of your trip, and the nature and length of your stay abroad.

To meet the bona fide residence test, you must show the IRS that you have been a bona fide resident of a foreign country or countries for an uninterrupted period that includes an entire tax year. The IRS decides whether you are a bona fide resident of a foreign country largely on the basis of facts you report on Form 2555. IRS cannot make this determination until you file Form 2555.

Statement to foreign authorities. You are not considered a bona fide resident of a foreign country if you make a statement to the authorities of that country that you are not a resident of that country, and the authorities:

● Hold that you are not subject to their income tax laws as a resident, or

● Have not made a final decision on your status.

Special agreements and treaties. An income tax exemption provided in a treaty or other international agreement will not in itself prevent you from being a bona fide resident of a foreign country. Whether a treaty prevents you from becoming a bona fide resident of a foreign country is determined under all provisions of the treaty, including specific provisions relating to residence or privileges and immunities.

Example 1. You are a U.S. citizen employed in the United Kingdom by a U.S. employer under contract with the U.S. Armed Forces. You are not subject to the North Atlantic Treaty Status of Forces Agreement. You may be a bona fide resident of the United Kingdom.

Example 2. You are a U.S. citizen in the United Kingdom who qualifies as an "employee" of an armed service or as a member of a "civilian component" under the North Atlantic Treaty Status of Forces Agreement. You are not a bona fide resident of the United Kingdom.

Example 3. You are a U.S. citizen employed in Japan by a U.S. employer under contract with the U.S. Armed Forces. You are subject to the agreement of the Treaty of Mutual Cooperation and Security between the United States and Japan. Being subject to the agreement does not make you a bona fide resident of Japan.

Example 4. You are a U.S. citizen employed as an "official" by the United Nations in Switzerland. You are exempt from Swiss taxation on the salary or wages paid to you by the United Nations. This does not prevent you from being a bona fide resident of Switzerland.

Effect of voting by absentee ballot. If you are a U.S. citizen living abroad, you can vote by absentee ballot in any election held in the United States without risking your status as a bona fide resident of a foreign country.

However, if you give information to the local election officials about the nature and length of your stay abroad that does not match the information you give for the bona fide residence test, the information given in connection with absentee voting will be considered in determining your status, but will not necessarily be conclusive.

Uninterrupted period including entire tax year. To meet the bona fide residence test, you must reside in a foreign country or countries for an uninterrupted period that includes an entire tax year. An entire tax year is from January 1 through December 31 for taxpayers who file their income tax returns on a calendar year basis.

During the period of bona fide residence in a foreign country, you can leave the country for brief or temporary trips back to the United States or elsewhere for vacation or business. To keep your status as a bona fide resident of a foreign country, you must have a clear intention of returning from such trips, without unreasonable delay, to your foreign residence or to a new bona fide residence in another foreign country.

Example 1. You arrived with your family in Lisbon, Portugal, on November 1, 2013. Your assignment is indefinite, and you intend to live there with your family until your company sends you to a new post. You immediately established residence there. You spent April of 2014 at a business conference in the United States. Your family stayed in Lisbon. Immediately following the conference, you returned to Lisbon and continued living there. On January 1, 2015, you completed an uninterrupted period of residence for a full tax year (2014), and you meet the bona fide residence test.

Example 2. Assume the same facts as in *Example 1,* except that you transferred back to the United States on December 13, 2014. You would not meet the bona fide residence test because your bona fide residence in the foreign country, although it lasted more than a year, did not include a full tax year. You may, however, qualify for the foreign earned income exclusion or the housing exclusion or deduction under the physical presence test (discussed later).

Bona fide resident for part of a year. Once you have established bona fide residence in a foreign country for an uninterrupted period that includes an entire tax year, you are a bona fide resident of that country for the period starting with the date you actually began the residence and ending with the date you abandon the foreign residence. Your period of bona fide residence can include an entire tax year plus parts of 2 other tax years.

Example. You were a bona fide resident of Singapore from March 1, 2013, through September 14, 2015. On September 15, 2015, you returned to the United States. Since you were a bona fide resident of a foreign country for all of 2014, you were also a bona fide resident of a foreign country from March 1, 2013, through the end of 2013 and from January 1, 2015, through September 14, 2015.

Reassignment. If you are assigned from one foreign post to another, you may or may not have a break in foreign residence between your assignments, depending on the circumstances.

Example 1. You were a resident of Pakistan from October 1, 2014, through November 30, 2015. On December 1, 2015, you and your family returned to the United States to wait for an assignment to another foreign country. Your

Figure 4–B. **How To Figure Overlapping 12-Month Periods**
This figure illustrates Example 2 under *How to figure the 12-month period.*

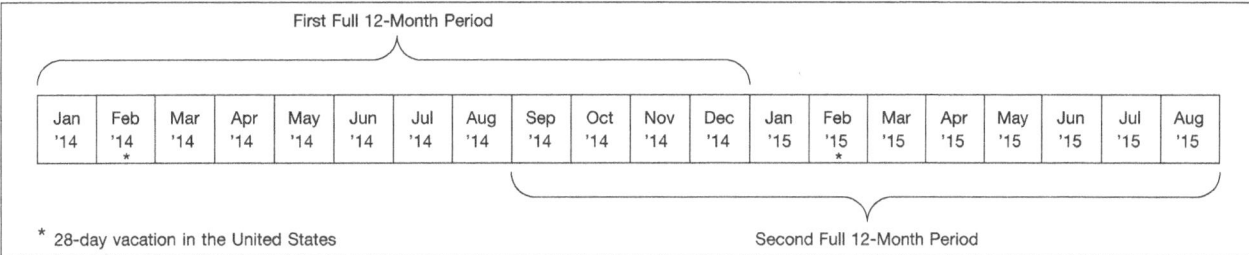

household goods also were returned to the United States.

Your foreign residence ended on November 30, 2015, and did not begin again until after you were assigned to another foreign country and physically entered that country. Since you were not a bona fide resident of a foreign country for the entire tax year of 2014 or 2015 you do not meet the bona fide residence test in either year. You may, however, qualify for the foreign earned income exclusion or the housing exclusion or deduction under the physical presence test, discussed later.

Example 2. Assume the same facts as in *Example 1,* except that upon completion of your assignment in Pakistan you were given a new assignment to Turkey. On December 1, 2015, you and your family returned to the United States for a month's vacation. On January 2, 2016, you arrived in Turkey for your new assignment. Because you did not interrupt your bona fide residence abroad, you meet the bona fide residence test.

Physical Presence Test

You meet the physical presence test if you are physically present in a foreign country or countries 330 full days during a period of 12 consecutive months. The 330 days do not have to be consecutive. Any U.S. citizen or resident alien can use the physical presence test to qualify for the exclusions and the deduction.

The physical presence test is based only on how long you stay in a foreign country or countries. This test does not depend on the kind of residence you establish, your intentions about returning, or the nature and purpose of your stay abroad.

330 full days. Generally, to meet the physical presence test, you must be physically present in a foreign country or countries for at least 330 full days during a 12-month period. You can count days you spent abroad for any reason. You do not have to be in a foreign country only for employment purposes. You can be on vacation.

You do not meet the physical presence test if illness, family problems, a vacation, or your employer's orders cause you to be present for less than the required amount of time.

Exception. You can be physically present in a foreign country or countries for less than 330 full days and still meet the physical presence test if you are required to leave a country

because of war or civil unrest. See *Waiver of Time Requirements,* later.

Full day. A full day is a period of 24 consecutive hours, beginning at midnight.

Travel. When you leave the United States to go directly to a foreign country or when you return directly to the United States from a foreign country, the time you spend on or over international waters does not count toward the 330-day total.

Example. You leave the United States for France by air on June 10. You arrive in France at 9:00 a.m. on June 11. Your first full day of physical presence in France is June 12.

Passing over foreign country. If, in traveling from the United States to a foreign country, you pass over a foreign country before midnight of the day you leave, the first day you can count toward the 330-day total is the day following the day you leave the United States.

Example. You leave the United States by air at 9:30 a.m. on June 10 to travel to Kenya. You pass over western Africa at 11:00 p.m. on June 10 and arrive in Kenya at 12:30 a.m. on June 11. Your first full day in a foreign country is June 11.

Change of location. You can move about from one place to another in a foreign country or to another foreign country without losing full days. If any part of your travel is not within any foreign country and takes less than 24 hours, you are considered to be in a foreign country during that part of travel.

Example 1. You leave Ireland by air at 11:00 p.m. on July 6 and arrive in Sweden at 5:00 a.m. on July 7. Your trip takes less than 24 hours and you lose no full days.

Example 2. You leave Norway by ship at 10:00 p.m. on July 6 and arrive in Portugal at 6:00 a.m. on July 8. Since your travel is not within a foreign country or countries and the trip takes more than 24 hours, you lose as full days July 6, 7, and 8. If you remain in Portugal, your next full day in a foreign country is July 9.

In United States while in transit. If you are in transit between two points outside the United States and are physically present in the United States for less than 24 hours, you are not treated as present in the United States during the transit. You are treated as traveling over areas not within any foreign country.

How to figure the 12-month period. There are four rules you should know when figuring the 12-month period.

- Your 12-month period can begin with any day of the month. It ends the day before the same calendar day, 12 months later.
- Your 12-month period must be made up of consecutive months. Any 12-month period can be used if the 330 days in a foreign country fall within that period.
- You do not have to begin your 12-month period with your first full day in a foreign country or end it with the day you leave. You can choose the 12-month period that gives you the greatest exclusion.
- In determining whether the 12-month period falls within a longer stay in the foreign country, 12-month periods can overlap one another.

Example 1. You are a construction worker who works on and off in a foreign country over a 20-month period. You might pick up the 330 full days in a 12-month period only during the middle months of the time you work in the foreign country because the first few and last few months of the 20-month period are broken up by long visits to the United States.

Example 2. You work in New Zealand for a 20-month period from January 1, 2014, through August 31, 2015, except that you spend 28 days in February 2014 and 28 days in February 2015 on vacation in the United States. You are present in New Zealand for at least 330 full days during each of the following two 12-month periods: January 1, 2014 – December 31, 2014 and September 1, 2014 – August 31, 2015. By overlapping the 12-month periods in this way, you meet the physical presence test for the whole 20-month period. See Figure 4-B, on the top of this page.

Waiver of Time Requirements

Both the bona fide residence test and the physical presence test contain minimum time requirements. The minimum time requirements can be waived, however, if you must leave a foreign country because of war, civil unrest, or similar adverse conditions in that country. You must be able to show that you reasonably could have expected to meet the minimum time requirements if not for the adverse conditions. To qualify for the waiver, you must actually have your tax home in the foreign country and be a bona fide resident of, or be physically present in, the foreign country on or before the beginning date of the waiver.

Early in 2016, the IRS will publish in the Internal Revenue Bulletin a list of the only countries that qualify for the waiver for 2015 and the effective dates. If you left one of the countries on or after the date listed for each country, you can meet the bona fide residence test or physical presence test for 2015 without meeting the minimum time requirement. However, in figuring your exclusion, the number of your qualifying days of bona fide residence or physical presence includes only days of actual residence or presence within the country.

Note. The countries and the respective dates that qualified for the waiver in 2014 are listed in Revenue Procedure 2015-25.

U.S. Travel Restrictions

If you are present in a foreign country in violation of U.S. law, you will not be treated as a bona fide resident of a foreign country or as physically present in a foreign country while you are in violation of the law. Income that you earn from sources within such a country for services performed during a period of violation does not qualify as foreign earned income. Your housing expenses within that country (or outside that country for housing your spouse or dependents) while you are in violation of the law cannot be included in figuring your foreign housing amount.

At the time this publication was released, the only country to which travel restrictions applied during 2015 was Cuba. However, individuals working at the U.S. Naval Base at Guantanamo Bay in Cuba are not in violation of U.S. law. Personal service income earned by individuals at the base is eligible for the foreign earned income exclusion provided the other requirements are met.

Foreign Earned Income

To claim the foreign earned income exclusion, the foreign housing exclusion, or the foreign housing deduction, you must have foreign earned income.

Foreign earned income generally is income you receive for services you perform during a period in which you meet both of the following requirements.
- Your tax home is in a foreign country.
- You meet either the bona fide residence test or the physical presence test.

To determine whether your tax home is in a foreign country, see *Tax Home in Foreign Country,* earlier. To determine whether you meet either the bona fide residence test or the physical presence test, see *Bona Fide Residence Test* and *Physical Presence Test*, earlier.

Foreign earned income does not include the following amounts.
- The value of meals and lodging that you exclude from your income because the meals and lodging were furnished for the convenience of your employer.

- Pension or annuity payments you receive, including social security benefits (see *Pensions and annuities,* later).
- Pay you receive as an employee of the U.S. Government. (See *U.S. Government Employees,* later.)
- Amounts you include in your income because of your employer's contributions to a nonexempt employee trust or to a nonqualified annuity contract.
- Any unallowable moving expense deduction that you choose to recapture as explained under *Moving Expense Attributable to Foreign Earnings in 2 Years* in chapter 5.
- Payments you receive after the end of the tax year following the tax year in which you performed the services that earned the income.

Earned income. This is pay for personal services performed, such as wages, salaries, or professional fees. The list that follows classifies many types of income into three categories. The column headed *Variable Income* lists income that may fall into either the earned income category, the unearned income category, or partly into both. For more information on earned and unearned income, see *Earned and Unearned Income*, later.

Earned Income	Unearned Income	Variable Income
Salaries and wages	Dividends	Business profits
Commissions	Interest	Royalties
Bonuses	Capital gains	Rents
Professional fees	Gambling winnings	Scholarships and fellowships
Tips	Alimony	
	Social security benefits	
	Pensions	
	Annuities	

In addition to the types of earned income listed, certain noncash income and allowances or reimbursements are considered earned income.

Noncash income. The fair market value of property or facilities provided to you by your employer in the form of lodging, meals, or use of a car is earned income.

Allowances or reimbursements. Earned income includes allowances or reimbursements you receive, such as the following amounts.
- Cost-of-living allowances.
- Overseas differential.
- Family allowance.
- Reimbursement for education or education allowance.
- Home leave allowance.
- Quarters allowance.
- Reimbursement for moving or moving allowance (unless excluded from income as

discussed later in *Reimbursement of employee expenses* under *Earned and Unearned Income*).

Source of Earned Income

The source of your earned income is the place where you perform the services for which you received the income. Foreign earned income is income you receive for working in a foreign country. Where or how you are paid has no effect on the source of the income. For example, income you receive for work done in Austria is income from a foreign source even if the income is paid directly to your bank account in the United States and your employer is located in New York City.

Example. You are a U.S. citizen, a bona fide resident of Canada, and working as a mining engineer. Your salary is $76,800 per year. You also receive a $6,000 cost-of-living allowance, and a $6,000 education allowance. Your employment contract did not indicate that you were entitled to these allowances only while outside the United States. Your total income is $88,800. You work a 5-day week, Monday through Friday. After subtracting your vacation, you have a total of 240 workdays in the year. You worked in the United States during the year for 6 weeks (30 workdays). The following shows how to figure the part of your income that is for work done in Canada during the year.

$$\frac{\text{Number of days worked in Canada during the year (210)}}{\text{Number of days of work during the year for which payment was made (240)}} \times \frac{\text{Total income}}{(\$88,800)} = \$77,700$$

Your foreign source earned income is $77,700.

Earned and Unearned Income

Earned income was defined earlier as pay for personal services performed. Some types of income are not easily identified as earned or unearned income. Some of these types of income are further explained here.

Income from a sole proprietorship or partnership. Income from a business in which capital investment is an important part of producing the income may be unearned income. If you are a sole proprietor or partner and your personal services are also an important part of producing the income, the part of the income that represents the value of your personal services will be treated as earned income.

Capital a factor. If capital investment is an important part of producing income, no more than 30% of your share of the net profits of the business is earned income.

If you have no net profits, the part of your gross profit that represents a reasonable allowance for personal services actually performed is considered earned income. Because you do not have a net profit, the 30% limit does not apply.

Example 1. You are a U.S. citizen and meet the bona fide residence test. You invest in a partnership based in Cameroon that is engaged solely in selling merchandise outside the United States. You perform no services for the partnership. At the end of the tax year, your share of the net profits is $80,000. The entire $80,000 is unearned income.

Example 2. Assume that in *Example 1* you spend time operating the business. Your share of the net profits is $80,000; 30% of your share of the profits is $24,000. If the value of your services for the year is $15,000, your earned income is limited to the value of your services, $15,000.

Capital not a factor. If capital is not an income-producing factor and personal services produce the business income, the 30% rule does not apply. The entire amount of business income is earned income.

Example. You and Lou Green are management consultants and operate as equal partners in performing services outside the United States. Because capital is not an income-producing factor, all the income from the partnership is considered earned income.

Income from a corporation. The salary you receive from a corporation is earned income only if it represents a reasonable allowance as compensation for work you do for the corporation. Any amount over what is considered a reasonable salary is unearned income.

Example 1. You are a U.S. citizen and an officer and stockholder of a corporation in Honduras. You perform no work or service of any kind for the corporation. During the tax year you receive a $10,000 "salary" from the corporation. The $10,000 clearly is not for personal services and is unearned income.

Example 2. You are a U.S. citizen and work full time as secretary-treasurer of your corporation. During the tax year you receive $100,000 as salary from the corporation. If $80,000 is a reasonable allowance as pay for the work you did, then $80,000 is earned income.

Stock options. You may have earned income if you disposed of stock that you got by exercising a stock option granted to you under an employee stock purchase plan.

If your gain on the disposition of stock you got by exercising an option is treated as capital gain, your gain is unearned income.

However, if you disposed of the stock less than 2 years after you were granted the option or less than 1 year after you got the stock, part of the gain on the disposition may be earned income. It is considered received in the year you

disposed of the stock and earned in the year you performed the services for which you were granted the option. Any part of the earned income that is due to work you did outside the United States is foreign earned income.

See Pub. 525, Taxable and Nontaxable Income, for a discussion of the treatment of stock options.

Pensions and annuities. For purposes of the foreign earned income exclusion, the foreign housing exclusion, and the foreign housing deduction, amounts received as pensions or annuities are unearned income.

Royalties. Royalties from the leasing of oil and mineral lands and patents generally are a form of rent or dividends and are unearned income.

Royalties received by a writer are earned income if they are received:

- For the transfer of property rights of the writer in the writer's product, or
- Under a contract to write a book or series of articles.

Rental income. Generally, rental income is unearned income. If you perform personal services in connection with the production of rent, up to 30% of your net rental income can be considered earned income.

Example. Larry Smith, a U.S. citizen living in Australia, owns and operates a rooming house in Sydney. If he is operating the rooming house as a business that requires capital and personal services, he can consider up to 30% of net rental income as earned income. On the other hand, if he just owns the rooming house and performs no personal services connected with its operation, except perhaps making minor repairs and collecting rents, none of his net income from the house is considered earned income. It is all unearned income.

Professional fees. If you are engaged in a professional occupation (such as a doctor or lawyer), all fees received in the performance of these services are earned income.

Income of an artist. Income you receive from the sale of paintings you created is earned income.

Scholarships and fellowships. Any portion of a scholarship or fellowship grant that is paid to you for teaching, research or other services is considered earned income if you must include it in your gross income. If the payer of the grant is required to provide you with a Form W-2, Wage and Tax Statement, these amounts will be listed as wages.

 Certain scholarship and fellowship income may be exempt under other provisions. See Pub. 970, Tax Benefits for Education, chapter 1.

Use of employer's property or facilities. If you receive fringe benefits in the form of the right to use your employer's property or facilities, the fair market value of that right is earned income. Fair market value is the price at which the property would change hands between a willing buyer and a willing seller, neither being

required to buy or sell, and both having reasonable knowledge of all the necessary facts.

Example. You are privately employed and live in Japan all year. You are paid a salary of $6,000 a month. You live rent-free in a house provided by your employer that has a fair rental value of $3,000 a month. The house is not provided for your employer's convenience. You report on the calendar-year, cash basis. You received $72,000 salary from foreign sources plus $36,000 fair rental value of the house, or a total of $108,000 of earned income.

Reimbursement of employee expenses. If you are reimbursed under an accountable plan (defined below) for expenses you incur on your employer's behalf and you have adequately accounted to your employer for the expenses, do not include the reimbursement for those expenses in your earned income.

The expenses for which you are reimbursed are not considered allocable (related) to your earned income. If expenses and reimbursement are equal, there is nothing to allocate to excluded income. If expenses are more than the reimbursement, the unreimbursed expenses are considered to have been incurred in producing earned income and must be divided between your excluded and included income in determining the amount of unreimbursed expenses you can deduct. (See chapter 5.) If the reimbursement is more than the expenses, no expenses remain to be divided between excluded and included income and the excess reimbursement must be included in earned income.

These rules do not apply to the following individuals.

- Straight-commission salespersons.
- Employees who have arrangements with their employers under which taxes are not withheld on a percentage of the commissions because the employers consider that percentage to be attributable to the employees' expenses.

Accountable plan. An accountable plan is a reimbursement or allowance arrangement that includes all three of the following rules.

- The expenses covered under the plan must have a business connection.
- The employee must adequately account to the employer for these expenses within a reasonable period of time.
- The employee must return any excess reimbursement or allowance within a reasonable period of time.

Reimbursement of moving expenses. Reimbursement of moving expenses may be earned income. You must include as earned income:

- Any reimbursements of, or payments for, nondeductible moving expenses,
- Reimbursements that are more than your deductible expenses and that you do not return to your employer,
- Any reimbursement made (or treated as made) under a nonaccountable plan (any plan that does not meet the rules listed above for an accountable plan), even if they are for deductible expenses, and
- Any reimbursement of moving expenses you deducted in an earlier year.

This section discusses reimbursements that must be included in earned income. Pub. 521, Moving Expenses, discusses additional rules that apply to moving expense deductions and reimbursements.

The rules for determining when the reimbursement is considered earned or where the reimbursement is considered earned may differ somewhat from the general rules previously discussed.

Although you receive the reimbursement in one tax year, it may be considered earned for services performed, or to be performed, in another tax year. You must report the reimbursement as income on your return in the year you receive it, even if it is considered earned during a different year.

Move from U.S. to foreign country. If you move from the United States to a foreign country, your moving expense reimbursement is generally considered pay for future services to be performed at the new location. The reimbursement is considered earned solely in the year of the move if you qualify for the exclusion for a period that includes at least 120 days during that tax year.

If you are neither a bona fide resident of nor physically present in a foreign country or countries for a period that includes 120 days during the year of the move, a portion of the reimbursement is considered earned in the year of the move and a portion is considered earned in the year following the year of the move. To figure the amount earned in the year of the move, multiply the reimbursement by a fraction. The numerator (top number) is the number of days in your qualifying period that fall within the year of the move, and the denominator (bottom number) is the total number of days in the year of the move.

The difference between the total reimbursement and the amount considered earned in the year of the move is the amount considered earned in the year following the year of the move. The part earned in each year is figured as shown in the following example.

Example. You are a U.S. citizen working in the United States. You were told in October 2014 that you were being transferred to a foreign country. You arrived in the foreign country on December 15, 2014, and you are a bona fide resident for the remainder of 2014 and all of 2015. Your employer reimbursed you $2,000 in January 2015 for the part of the moving expense that you were not allowed to deduct. Because you did not qualify for the exclusion under the bona fide residence test for at least 120 days in 2014 (the year of the move), the reimbursement is considered pay for services performed in the foreign country for both 2014 and 2015.

You figure the part of the reimbursement for services performed in the foreign country in 2014 by multiplying the total reimbursement by a fraction. The fraction is the number of days during which you were a bona fide resident in 2014 (the year of the move) divided by 365. The remaining part of the reimbursement is for services performed in the foreign country in 2015.

This computation is used only to determine when the reimbursement is considered earned. You would include the amount of the reimbursement in income in 2015, the year you received it.

Move between foreign countries. If you move between foreign countries, any moving expense reimbursement that you must include in income will be considered earned in the year of the move if you qualify for the foreign earned income exclusion for a period that includes at least 120 days in the year of the move.

Move to U.S. If you move to the United States, the moving expense reimbursement that you must include in income is generally considered to be U.S. source income.

However, if under either an agreement between you and your employer or a statement of company policy that is reduced to writing before your move to the foreign country, your employer will reimburse you for your move back to the United States regardless of whether you continue to work for the employer, the includible reimbursement is considered compensation for past services performed in the foreign country. The includible reimbursement is considered earned in the year of the move if you qualify for the foreign earned income exclusion for a period that includes at least 120 days during that year. Otherwise, you treat the includible reimbursement as received for services performed in the foreign country in the year of the move and the year immediately before the year of the move.

See the discussion under *Move from U.S. to foreign country*, earlier, to figure the amount of the includible reimbursement considered earned in the year of the move. The amount earned in the year before the year of the move is the difference between the total includible reimbursement and the amount earned in the year of the move.

Example. You are a U.S. citizen employed in a foreign country. You retired from employment with your employer on March 31, 2015, and returned to the United States after having been a bona fide resident of the foreign country for several years. A written agreement with your employer entered into before you went abroad provided that you would be reimbursed for your move back to the United States.

In April 2015, your former employer reimbursed you $4,000 for the part of the cost of your move back to the United States that you were not allowed to deduct. Because you were not a bona fide resident of a foreign country or countries for a period that included at least 120 days in 2015 (the year of the move), the includible reimbursement is considered pay for services performed in the foreign country for both 2015 and 2014.

You figure the part of the moving expense reimbursement for services performed in the foreign country for 2015 by multiplying the total includible reimbursement by a fraction. The fraction is the number of days of foreign residence during the year (90) divided by the number of days in the year (365). The remaining part of the includible reimbursement is for services performed in the foreign country in 2014. You report the amount of the includible reimbursement in 2015, the year you received it.

 In this example, if you met the physical presence test for a period that included at least 120 days in 2015, the moving expense reimbursement would be considered earned entirely in the year of the move.

Storage expense reimbursements. If you are reimbursed for storage expenses, the reimbursement is for services you perform during the period of time for which the storage expenses are incurred.

U.S. Government Employees

For purposes of the foreign earned income exclusion, the foreign housing exclusion, and the foreign housing deduction, foreign earned income does not include any amounts paid by the United States or any of its agencies to its employees. This includes amounts paid from both appropriated and nonappropriated funds.

The following organizations (and other organizations similarly organized and operated under United States Army, Navy, or Air Force regulations) are integral parts of the Armed Forces, agencies, or instrumentalities of the United States.

- United States Armed Forces exchanges.
- Commissioned and noncommissioned officers' messes.
- Armed Forces motion picture services.
- Kindergartens on foreign Armed Forces installations.

Amounts paid by the United States or its agencies to persons who are not their employees may qualify for exclusion or deduction.

If you are a U.S. Government employee paid by a U.S. agency that assigned you to a foreign government to perform specific services for which the agency is reimbursed by the foreign government, your pay is from the U.S. Government and does not qualify for exclusion or deduction.

If you have questions about whether you are an employee or an independent contractor, get Pub. 15-A, Employer's Supplemental Tax Guide.

American Institute in Taiwan. Amounts paid by the American Institute in Taiwan are not foreign earned income for purposes of the foreign earned income exclusion, the foreign housing exclusion, or the foreign housing deduction. If you are an employee of the American Institute in Taiwan, allowances you receive are exempt from U.S. tax up to the amount that equals tax-exempt allowances received by civilian employees of the U.S. Government.

Allowances. Cost-of-living and foreign-area allowances paid under certain acts of Congress to U.S. civilian officers and employees stationed in Alaska and Hawaii or elsewhere outside the 48 contiguous states and the District of Columbia can be excluded from gross income. Post differentials are wages that must be included in gross income, regardless of the act of Congress under which they are paid.

More information. Pub. 516, U.S. Government Civilian Employees Stationed Abroad, has more information for U.S. Government employees abroad.

Exclusion of Meals and Lodging

You do not include in your income the value of meals and lodging provided to you and your family by your employer at no charge if the following conditions are met.

1. The meals are furnished:
    a. On the business premises of your employer, and
    b. For the convenience of your employer.
2. The lodging is furnished:
    a. On the business premises of your employer,
    b. For the convenience of your employer, and
    c. As a condition of your employment.

If these conditions are met, do not include the value of the meals or lodging in your income, even if a law or your employment contract says that they are provided as compensation.

Amounts you do not include in income because of these rules are not foreign earned income.

If you receive a Form W-2, excludable amounts should not be included in the total reported in box 1 as wages.

Family. Your family, for this purpose, includes only your spouse and your dependents.

Lodging. The value of lodging includes the cost of heat, electricity, gas, water, sewer service, and similar items needed to make the lodging fit to live in.

Business premises of employer. Generally, the business premises of your employer is wherever you work. For example, if you work as a housekeeper, meals and lodging provided in your employer's home are provided on the business premises of your employer. Similarly, meals provided to cowhands while herding cattle on land leased or owned by their employer are considered provided on the premises of their employer.

Convenience of employer. Whether meals or lodging are provided for your employer's convenience must be determined from all the facts and circumstances. Meals furnished at no charge are considered provided for your employer's convenience if there is a good business reason for providing them, other than to give you more pay.

On the other hand, if your employer provides meals to you or your family as a means of giving you more pay, and there is no other business reason for providing them, their value is extra income to you because they are not furnished for the convenience of your employer.

Condition of employment. Lodging is provided as a condition of employment if you must accept the lodging to properly carry out the duties of your job. You must accept lodging to properly carry out your duties if, for example, you must be available for duty at all times or you could not perform your duties if the lodging was not furnished.

Foreign camps. If the lodging is in a camp located in a foreign country, the camp is considered part of your employer's business premises. The camp must be:

● Provided for your employer's convenience because the place where you work is in a remote area where satisfactory housing is not available to you on the open market within a reasonable commuting distance,
● Located as close as reasonably possible in the area where you work, and
● Provided in a common area or enclave that is not available to the general public for lodging or accommodations and that normally houses at least ten employees.

Foreign Earned Income Exclusion

If your tax home is in a foreign country and you meet the bona fide residence test or the physical presence test, you can choose to exclude from your income a limited amount of your foreign earned income. Foreign earned income was defined earlier in this chapter.

You also can choose to exclude from your income a foreign housing amount. This is explained later under *Foreign Housing Exclusion*. If you choose to exclude a foreign housing amount, you must figure the foreign housing exclusion before you figure the foreign earned income exclusion. Your foreign earned income exclusion is limited to your foreign earned income minus your foreign housing exclusion.

If you choose to exclude foreign earned income, you cannot deduct, exclude, or claim a credit for any item that can be allocated to or charged against the excluded amounts. This includes any expenses, losses, and other normally deductible items allocable to the excluded income. For more information about deductions and credits, see *chapter 5*.

Limit on Excludable Amount

You may be able to exclude up to $100,800 of your foreign earned income in 2015.

You cannot exclude more than the smaller of:

● $100,800, or
● Your foreign earned income (discussed earlier) for the tax year minus your foreign housing exclusion (discussed later).

If both you and your spouse work abroad and each of you meets either the bona fide residence test or the physical presence test, you can each choose the foreign earned income exclusion. You do not both need to meet the same test. Together, you and your spouse can exclude as much as $201,600.

Paid in year following work. Generally, you are considered to have earned income in the year in which you do the work for which you receive the income, even if you work in one year but are not paid until the following year. If you report your income on a cash basis, you report the income on your return for the year you receive it. If you work one year, but are not paid for that work until the next year, the amount you can exclude in the year you are paid is the amount you could have excluded in the year you did the work if you had been paid in that year. For an exception to this general rule, see *Year-end payroll period*, later.

Example. You were a bona fide resident of Brazil for all of 2014 and 2015. You report your income on the cash basis. In 2014, you were paid $87,400 for work you did in Brazil during that year. You excluded all of the $87,400 from your income in 2014.

In 2015, you were paid $120,500 for your work in Brazil. $20,500 was for work you did in 2014 and $100,000 was for work you did in 2015. You can exclude $11,800 of the $20,500 from your income in 2015. This is the $99,200 maximum exclusion in 2014 minus the $87,400 actually excluded that year. You must include the remaining $8,700 in income in 2015 because you could not have excluded that income in 2014 if you had received it that year. You can exclude all of the $100,000 you were paid for work you did in 2015 from your 2015 income.

Your total foreign earned income exclusion for 2015 is $111,800 ($11,800 for work you did in 2014 and $100,000 for work you did in 2015). You would include in your 2015 income $8,700 for the work you did in 2014.

Year-end payroll period. There is an exception to the general rule that income is considered earned in the year you do the work for which you receive the income. If you are a cash-basis taxpayer, any salary or wage payment you receive after the end of the year in which you do the work for which you receive the pay is considered earned entirely in the year you receive it if all four of the following apply.

● The period for which the payment is made is a normal payroll period of your employer that regularly applies to you.
● The payroll period includes the last day of your tax year (December 31 if you figure your taxes on a calendar-year basis).
● The payroll period is not longer than 16 days.
● The payday comes at the same time in relation to the payroll period that it would normally come and it comes before the end of the next payroll period.

Example. You are paid twice a month. For the normal payroll period that begins on the first of the month and ends on the fifteenth of the month, you are paid on the sixteenth day of the month. For the normal payroll period that begins on the sixteenth of the month and ends on the last day of the month, you are paid on the first day of the following month. Because all of the above conditions are met, the pay you received on January 1, 2015, is considered earned in 2015.

Income earned over more than 1 year. Regardless of when you actually receive income, you must apply it to the year in which you earned it in figuring your excludable amount for that year. For example, a bonus may be based on work you did over several years. You determine the amount of the bonus that is considered earned in a particular year in two steps.

1. Divide the bonus by the number of calendar months in the period when you did the work that resulted in the bonus.

2. Multiply the result of (1) by the number of months you did the work during the year. This is the amount that is subject to the exclusion limit for that tax year.

Income received more than 1 year after it was earned. You cannot exclude income you receive after the end of the year following the year you do the work to earn it.

Example. You were a bona fide resident of Sweden for 2013, 2014, and 2015. You report your income on the cash basis. In 2013, you were paid $69,000 for work you did in Sweden that year and in 2014 you were paid $74,000 for that year's work in Sweden. You excluded all the income on your 2013 and 2014 returns.

In 2015, you were paid $92,000; $82,000 for your work in Sweden during 2015, and $10,000 for work you did in Sweden in 2013. You cannot exclude any of the $10,000 for work done in 2013 because you received it after the end of the year following the year in which you earned it. You must include the $10,000 in income. You can exclude all of the $82,000 received for work you did in 2015.

Community income. The maximum exclusion applies separately to the earnings of spouses. Ignore any community property laws when you figure your limit on the foreign earned income exclusion.

Part-year exclusion. If the period for which you qualify for the foreign earned income exclusion includes only part of the year, you must adjust the maximum limit based on the number of qualifying days in the year. The number of qualifying days is the number of days in the year within the period on which you both:
- Have your tax home in a foreign country, and
- Meet either the bona fide residence test or the physical presence test.

For this purpose, you can count as qualifying days all days within a period of 12 consecutive months once you are physically present and have your tax home in a foreign country for 330 full days. To figure your maximum exclusion, multiply the maximum excludable amount for the year by the number of your qualifying days in the year, and then divide the result by the number of days in the year.

Example. You report your income on the calendar-year basis and you qualified for the foreign earned income exclusion under the bona fide residence test for 75 days in 2015.

You can exclude a maximum of 75/365 of $100,800, or $20,712, of your foreign earned income for 2015. If you qualify under the bona fide residence test for all of 2016, you can exclude your foreign earned income up to the 2016 limit.

Physical presence test. Under the physical presence test, a 12-month period can be any period of 12 consecutive months that includes 330 full days. If you qualify for the foreign earned income exclusion under the physical presence test for part of a year, it is important to carefully choose the 12-month period that will allow the maximum exclusion for that year.

Example. You are physically present and have your tax home in a foreign country for a 16-month period from June 1, 2014, through September 30, 2015, except for 16 days in December 2014 when you were on vacation in the United States. You figure the maximum exclusion for 2014 as follows.

1. Beginning with June 1, 2014, count forward 330 full days. Do not count the 16 days you spent in the United States. The 330th day, May 12, 2015, is the last day of a 12-month period.

2. Count backward 12 months from May 11, 2015, to find the first day of this 12-month period, May 12, 2014. This 12-month period runs from May 12, 2014, through May 11, 2015.

3. Count the total days during 2014 that fall within this 12-month period. This is 234 days (May 12, 2014 – December 31, 2014).

4. Multiply $99,200 (the maximum exclusion for 2014) by the fraction 234/365 to find your maximum exclusion for 2014 ($63,597).

You figure the maximum exclusion for 2015 in the opposite manner.

1. Beginning with your last full day, September 30, 2015, count backward 330 full days. Do not count the 16 days you spent in the United States. That day, October 20, 2014, is the first day of a 12-month period.

2. Count forward 12 months from October 20, 2014, to find the last day of this 12-month period, October 19, 2015. This 12-month period runs from October 20, 2014, through October 19, 2015.

3. Count the total days during 2015 that fall within this 12-month period. This is 292 days (January 1, 2015 – October 19, 2015).

4. Multiply $100,800, the maximum limit, by the fraction 292/365 to find your maximum exclusion for 2015 ($80,640).

Choosing the Exclusion

The foreign earned income exclusion is voluntary. You can choose the exclusion by completing the appropriate parts of Form 2555 or Form 2555-EZ.

When You Can Choose the Exclusion

Your initial choice of the exclusion on Form 2555 or Form 2555-EZ generally must be made with one of the following returns.
- A return filed by the due date (including any extensions).
- A return amending a timely-filed return. Amended returns generally must be filed by the later of 3 years after the filing date of the original return or 2 years after the tax is paid.
- A return filed within 1 year from the original due date of the return (determined without regard to any extensions).

Filing after the above periods. You can choose the exclusion on a return filed after the periods described above if you owe no federal income tax after taking into account the exclusion. If you owe federal income tax after taking into account the exclusion, you can choose the exclusion on a return filed after the periods described earlier if you file before the IRS discovers that you failed to choose the exclusion. Whether or not you owe federal income tax after taking the exclusion into account, if you file your return after the periods described earlier, you must type or legibly print at the top of the first page of the Form 1040 "Filed pursuant to section 1.911-7(a)(2)(i)(D)."

If you owe federal income tax after taking into account the foreign earned income exclusion and the IRS discovered that you failed to choose the exclusion, you may still be able to choose the exclusion. You must request a private letter ruling under Income Tax Regulation 301.9100-3 and Revenue Procedure 2015-1, 2015-1 I.R.B. 1, available at *www.irs.gov/irb/2015-1_IRB/ar07.html*.

Effect of Choosing the Exclusion

Once you choose to exclude your foreign earned income, that choice remains in effect for that year and all later years unless you revoke it.

Foreign tax credit or deduction. Once you choose to exclude foreign earned income, you cannot take a foreign tax credit or deduction for taxes on income you can exclude. If you do take a credit or deduction for any of those taxes in a subsequent year, your election for the foreign earned income exclusion will be revoked beginning with that year. See Pub. 514, for more information.

Additional child tax credit. You cannot take the additional child tax credit if you claim the foreign earned income exclusion.

Earned income credit. If you claim the foreign earned income exclusion, you will not qualify for the earned income credit for the year. For more information on this credit, see Pub. 596.

Figuring tax on income not excluded. If you claim the foreign earned income exclusion, the housing exclusion (discussed later), or both, you must figure the tax on your nonexcluded income using the tax rates that would have applied had you not claimed the exclusions. See the instructions for Form 1040 and complete the *Foreign Earned Income Tax Worksheet* to figure the amount of tax to enter on Form 1040, line 44. If you must attach Form 6251, Alternative Minimum Tax — Individuals, to your return, use the *Foreign Earned Income Tax Worksheet* provided in the instructions for Form 6251.

Revoking the Exclusion

You can revoke your choice for any year. You do this by attaching a statement that you are revoking one or more previously made choices to the return or amended return for the first year that you do not wish to claim the exclusion(s). You must specify which choice(s) you are revoking. You must revoke separately a choice to exclude foreign earned income and a choice to exclude foreign housing amounts.

If you revoked a choice and within 5 years again wish to choose the same exclusion, you must apply for IRS approval. You do this by requesting a ruling from the IRS.

 Mail your request for a ruling, in duplicate, to:

Associate Chief Counsel (International)
Internal Revenue Service
Attn: CC:PA:LPD:DRU
P.O. Box 7604
Ben Franklin Station
Washington, DC 20044

Because requesting a ruling can be complex, you may need professional help. Also, the IRS charges a fee for issuing these rulings. For more information, see Revenue Procedure 2015-1.

In deciding whether to give approval, the IRS will consider any facts and circumstances that may be relevant. These may include a period of residence in the United States, a move from one foreign country to another foreign country with different tax rates, a substantial change in the tax laws of the foreign country of residence or physical presence, and a change of employer.

Foreign Housing Exclusion and Deduction

In addition to the foreign earned income exclusion, you also can claim an exclusion or a deduction from gross income for your housing amount if your tax home is in a foreign country and you qualify for the exclusions and deduction under either the bona fide residence test or the physical presence test.

The housing exclusion applies only to amounts considered paid for with employer-provided amounts. The housing deduction applies only to amounts paid for with self-employment earnings.

If you are married and you and your spouse each qualifies under one of the tests, see *Married Couples,* later.

Housing Amount

Your housing amount is the total of your housing expenses for the year minus the base housing amount.

Base housing amount. The computation of the base housing amount (line 32 of Form 2555) is tied to the maximum foreign earned income exclusion. The amount is 16% of the exclusion amount (computed on a daily basis), multiplied by the number of days in your qualifying period that fall within your tax year.

For 2015, the maximum foreign earned income exclusion is $100,800 per year; 16% of this amount is $16,128, or $44.19 per day. To figure your base housing amount if you are a calendar-year taxpayer, multiply $44.19 by the number of your qualifying days during 2015. (See *Part-year exclusion* under *Limit on Excludable Amount,* earlier.) Subtract the result from your total housing expenses (up to the applicable limit) to find your housing amount.

Example. Your qualifying period includes all of 2015. During the year, you spent $18,628 for your housing. This is below the limit for the location in which you incurred the expenses. Your housing amount is $18,628 minus $16,128, or $2,500.

U.S. Government allowance. You must reduce your housing amount by any U.S. Government allowance or similar nontaxable allowance intended to compensate you or your spouse for the expenses of housing during the period for which you claim a foreign housing exclusion or deduction.

Housing expenses. Housing expenses include your reasonable expenses paid or incurred for housing in a foreign country for you and (if they live with you) for your spouse and dependents.

Consider only housing expenses for the part of the year that you qualify for the foreign earned income exclusion.

Housing expenses include:
- Rent,
- The fair rental value of housing provided in kind by your employer,
- Repairs,
- Utilities (other than telephone charges),
- Real and personal property insurance,
- Nondeductible occupancy taxes,
- Nonrefundable fees for securing a leasehold,
- Rental of furniture and accessories, and
- Residential parking.

Housing expenses do not include:
- Expenses that are lavish or extravagant under the circumstances,
- Deductible interest and taxes (including deductible interest and taxes of a tenant-stockholder in a cooperative housing corporation),
- The cost of buying property, including principal payments on a mortgage,
- The cost of domestic labor (maids, gardeners, etc.),
- Pay television subscriptions,
- Improvements and other expenses that increase the value or appreciably prolong the life of property,
- Purchased furniture or accessories, or
- Depreciation or amortization of property or improvements.

 No double benefit. You cannot include in housing expenses the value of meals or lodging that you exclude from gross income (see Exclusion of Meals and Lodging, earlier) or that you deduct as moving expenses.

Limit on housing expenses. The amount of qualified housing expenses eligible for the housing exclusion and housing deduction is limited. The limit is generally 30% of the maximum foreign earned income exclusion (computed on a daily basis), multiplied by the number of days in your qualifying period that fall within your tax year. For 2015, this is generally $82.85 per day ($30,240 per year). However, the limit will vary depending upon the location of your foreign tax home.

A qualified individual incurring housing expenses in a high-cost locality during 2015 can use housing expenses that total more than the standard limit on housing expenses ($30,240) to determine the housing amount. An individual who does not incur housing expenses in a high-cost locality is limited to maximum housing expenses of $82.85 per day ($30,240 per year).

The limits for high-cost localities are listed in the Instructions for Form 2555.

 You can elect to apply the 2015 housing cost limits to figure your 2014 housing exclusion instead of using the 2014 limits. The IRS and Treasury anticipate that you will be able to elect to apply the 2016 limits to figure your 2015 housing exclusion instead of using the 2015 limits.

Second foreign household. Ordinarily, if you maintain two foreign households, your reasonable foreign housing expenses include only costs for the household that bears the closer relationship (not necessarily geographic) to your tax home. However, if you maintain a second, separate household outside the United States for your spouse or dependents because living conditions near your tax home are dangerous, unhealthful, or otherwise adverse, include the expenses for the second household in your reasonable foreign housing expenses. You cannot include expenses for more than one second foreign household at the same time.

If you maintain two households and you exclude the value of one because it is provided by your employer, you can still include the expenses for the second household in figuring a foreign housing exclusion or deduction.

Adverse living conditions include:

- A state of warfare or civil insurrection in the general area of your tax home, and
- Conditions under which it is not feasible to provide family housing (for example, if you must live on a construction site or drilling rig).

Foreign Housing Exclusion

If you do not have self-employment income, all of your earnings are employer-provided amounts and your entire housing amount is considered paid for with those employer-provided amounts. This means that you can exclude (up to the limits) your entire housing amount.

Employer-provided amounts. These include any amounts paid to you or paid or incurred on your behalf by your employer that are taxable foreign earned income (without regard to the foreign earned income exclusion) to you for the year. Employer-provided amounts include:

- Your salary,
- Any reimbursement for housing expenses,
- Amounts your employer pays to a third party on your behalf,
- The fair rental value of company-owned housing furnished to you unless that value is excluded under the rules explained earlier at *Exclusion of Meals and Lodging*,
- Amounts paid to you by your employer as part of a tax equalization plan, and
- Amounts paid to you or a third party by your employer for the education of your dependents.

Choosing the exclusion. You can choose the housing exclusion by completing the appropriate parts of Form 2555. You cannot use Form 2555-EZ to claim the housing exclusion. Otherwise, the rules about choosing the exclusion under *Foreign Earned Income Exclusion* also apply to the foreign housing exclusion.

Your housing exclusion is the lesser of:

- That part of your housing amount paid for with employer-provided amounts, or
- Your foreign earned income.

If you choose the housing exclusion, you must figure it before figuring your foreign earned income exclusion. You cannot claim less than the full amount of the housing exclusion to which you are entitled.

Figuring tax on income not excluded. If you claim the housing exclusion, the foreign earned income exclusion (discussed earlier), or both, you must figure the tax on your nonexcluded income using the tax rates that would have applied had you not claimed the exclusions. See the instructions for Form 1040 and complete the *Foreign Earned Income Tax Worksheet* to figure the amount of tax to enter on Form 1040, line 44. If you must attach Form 6251 to your return, use the *Foreign Earned Income Tax Worksheet* provided in the instructions for Form 6251.

Foreign tax credit or deduction. Once you choose to exclude foreign housing amounts, you cannot take a foreign tax credit or deduction for taxes on income you can exclude. If you do take a credit or deduction for any of those taxes, your choice to exclude housing amounts may be considered revoked. See Pub. 514 for more information.

Additional child tax credit You cannot take the additional child tax credit if you claim the foreign housing exclusion.

Earned income credit. If you claim the foreign housing exclusion, you will not qualify for the earned income credit for the year.

Foreign Housing Deduction

If you do not have self-employment income, you cannot take a foreign housing deduction.

How you figure your housing deduction depends on whether you have only self-employment income or both self-employment income and employer-provided income. In either case, the amount you can deduct is subject to the limit described later.

Self-employed — no employer-provided amounts. If none of your housing amount is considered paid for with employer-provided amounts, such as when all of your income is from self-employment, you can deduct your housing amount, subject to the limit described later.

Take the deduction by including it in the total on line 36 of Form 1040. On the dotted line next to line 36, enter the amount and write "Form 2555."

Self-employed and employer-provided amounts. If you are both an employee and a self-employed individual during the year, you can deduct part of your housing amount and exclude part of it. To find the part that you can exclude, multiply your housing amount by the employer-provided amounts (discussed earlier) and then divide the result by your foreign earned income. This is the amount you can use to figure your foreign housing exclusion. You can deduct the balance of the housing amount, subject to the limit described later.

Example. Your housing amount for the year is $12,000. During the year, your total foreign earned income is $80,000, of which half ($40,000) is from self-employment and half is from your services as an employee. Half of your housing amount ($12,000 ÷ 2) is considered provided by your employer. You can exclude $6,000 as a housing exclusion. You can deduct the remaining $6,000 as a housing deduction subject to the following limit.

Limit

Your housing deduction cannot be more than your foreign earned income minus the total of:

- Your foreign earned income exclusion, plus
- Your housing exclusion.

Carryover. You can carry over to the next year any part of your housing deduction that is not allowed because of the limit. You are allowed to carry over your excess housing deduction to the next year only. If you cannot deduct it in the next year, you cannot carry it over to any other year. You deduct the carryover in figuring adjusted gross income. The amount of carryover you can deduct is limited to your foreign earned income for the year of the carryover minus the total of your foreign earned income exclusion, housing exclusion, and housing deduction for that year.

Additional child tax credit. You cannot take the additional child tax credit if you claim the foreign housing deduction.

Married Couples

If both you and your spouse qualify for the foreign housing exclusion or the foreign housing deduction, how you figure the benefits depends on whether you maintain separate households.

Separate Households

If you and your spouse live apart and maintain separate households, you both may be able to claim the foreign housing exclusion or the foreign housing deduction. You both can claim the exclusion or the deduction if both of the following conditions are met.

- You and your spouse have different tax homes that are not within reasonable commuting distance of each other.
- Neither spouse's residence is within reasonable commuting distance of the other spouse's tax home.

Housing exclusion. Each spouse claiming a housing exclusion must figure separately the part of the housing amount that is attributable to employer-provided amounts, based on his or her separate foreign earned income.

One Household

If you and your spouse lived in the same foreign household and file a joint return, you must figure your housing amounts jointly. If you file separate returns, only one spouse can claim the housing exclusion or deduction.

In figuring your housing amount jointly, you can combine your housing expenses and figure one base housing amount. Either spouse (but not both) can claim the housing exclusion or housing deduction. However, if you and your spouse have different periods of residence or presence and the one with the shorter period of residence or presence claims the exclusion or deduction, you can claim as housing expenses only the expenses for that shorter period.

Example. Tom and Jane live together and file a joint return. Tom was a bona fide resident of and had his tax home in Ghana from August 17, 2015, through December 31, 2016. Jane was a bona fide resident of and had her tax home in Ghana from September 15, 2015, through December 31, 2016.

During 2015, Tom received $75,000 of foreign earned income and Jane received $50,000 of foreign earned income. Tom paid $10,000 for housing expenses, of which $7,500 was for expenses incurred from September 15 through the end of the year. Jane paid $3,000 for housing expenses in 2015, all of which were incurred during her period of residence in Ghana.

Tom and Jane figure their housing amount jointly. If Tom claims the housing exclusion, their housing expenses would be $13,000 and their base housing amount, using Tom's 2015 period of residence (Aug. 17 – Dec. 31, 2015), would be $6,054 ($44.19 × 137 days). Tom's housing amount would be $6,946 ($13,000 – $6,054). If, instead, Jane claims the housing exclusion, their housing expenses would be limited to $10,500 ($7,500 + $3,000) and their base housing amount, using Jane's period of residence (Sept. 15 – Dec. 31, 2015), would be $4,773 ($44.19 × 108 days). Jane's housing amount would be $5,727 ($10,500 – $4,773).

Form 2555 and Form 2555-EZ

If you are claiming the foreign earned income exclusion only, you can use Form 2555. In some circumstances, you can use Form 2555-EZ to claim the foreign earned income exclusion. You must file one of these forms each year you are claiming the exclusion.

If you are claiming either the foreign housing exclusion or the foreign housing deduction, you must use Form 2555. You cannot use Form 2555-EZ. Form 2555 shows how you meet the bona fide residence test or physical presence test, how much of your earned income is excluded, and how to figure the amount of your allowable housing exclusion or deduction.

Do not submit Form 2555 or Form 2555-EZ by itself.

Form 2555-EZ

Form 2555-EZ has fewer lines than Form 2555. You can use this form if all seven of the following apply.
- You are a U.S. citizen or a resident alien.
- Your total foreign earned income for the year is $100,800 or less.
- You have earned wages/salaries in a foreign country.
- You are filing a calendar year return that covers a 12-month period.
- You did not have any self-employment income for the year.
- You did not have any business or moving expenses for the year.
- You are not claiming the foreign housing exclusion or deduction.

Form 2555

If you claim exclusion under the bona fide residence test, you should fill out Parts I, II, IV, and V of Form 2555. In filling out Part II, be sure to give your visa type and the period of your bona fide residence. Frequently, these items are overlooked.

If you claim exclusion under the physical presence test, you should fill out Parts I, III, IV, and V of Form 2555. When filling out Part III, be sure to insert the beginning and ending dates of your 12-month period and the dates of your arrivals and departures, as requested in the travel schedule.

You must fill out Part VI if you are claiming a foreign housing exclusion or deduction.

Fill out Part IX if you are claiming the foreign housing deduction.

If you are claiming the foreign earned income exclusion, fill out Part VII.

Finally, if you are claiming the foreign earned income exclusion, the foreign housing exclusion, or both, fill out Part VIII.

If you and your spouse both qualify to claim the foreign earned income exclusion, the foreign housing exclusion, or the foreign housing deduction, you and your spouse must file separate Forms 2555 to claim these benefits. See the discussion earlier under *Separate House-holds*.

5.

Exemptions, Deductions, and Credits

Topics
This chapter discusses:

- The rules concerning items related to excluded income,
- Exemptions,
- Contributions to foreign charitable organizations,
- Moving expenses,
- Contributions to individual retirement arrangements (IRAs),
- Taxes of foreign countries and U.S. possessions, and
- How to report deductions.

Useful Items
You may want to see:

Publication
- ❑ **501** Exemptions, Standard Deduction, and Filing Information
- ❑ **514** Foreign Tax Credit for Individuals
- ❑ **521** Moving Expenses
- ❑ **523** Selling Your Home
- ❑ **590-A** Contributions to Individual Retirement Arrangements (IRAs)

- ❑ **597** Information on the United States—Canada Income Tax Treaty

Form (and Instructions)
- ❑ **1116** Foreign Tax Credit
- ❑ **2106** Employee Business Expenses
- ❑ **2555** Foreign Earned Income
- ❑ **2555-EZ** Foreign Earned Income Exclusion
- ❑ **3903** Moving Expenses
- ❑ **Schedule A (Form 1040)** Itemized Deductions
- ❑ **Schedule C (Form 1040)** Profit or Loss From Business
- ❑ **SS-5** Application for a Social Security Card
- ❑ **W-7** Application for IRS Individual Taxpayer Identification Number

See chapter 7 for information about getting these publications and forms.

Items Related to Excluded Income

U.S. citizens and resident aliens living outside the United States generally are allowed the same deductions as citizens and residents living in the United States.

If you choose to exclude foreign earned income or housing amounts, you cannot deduct, exclude, or claim a credit for any item that can be allocated to or charged against the excluded amounts. This includes any expenses, losses, and other normally deductible items that are allocable to the excluded income. You can deduct only those expenses connected with earning includible income.

These rules apply only to items definitely related to the excluded earned income and they do not apply to other items that are not definitely related to any particular type of gross income. These rules do not apply to items such as:
- Personal exemptions,
- Qualified retirement contributions,
- Alimony payments,
- Charitable contributions,
- Medical expenses,
- Mortgage interest, or
- Real estate taxes on your personal residence.

For purposes of these rules, your housing deduction is not treated as allocable to your excluded income, but the deduction for self-employment tax is.

If you receive foreign earned income in a tax year after the year in which you earned it, you may have to file an amended return for the earlier year to properly adjust the amounts of deductions, credits, or exclusions allocable to your foreign earned income and housing exclusions.

Example. In 2014, you had $92,000 of foreign earned income and $9,500 of deductions allocable to your foreign earned income. You did not have a housing exclusion. Because you excluded all of your foreign earned income, you would not have been able to claim any of the deductions on your 2014 return.

In 2015, you received a $13,500 bonus for work you did abroad in 2014. You can exclude $7,200 of the bonus because the limit on the foreign earned income exclusion for 2014 was $99,200 and you have already excluded $92,000. Since you must include $6,300 of the bonus ($13,500 − $7,200) for work you did in 2014 in income, you can file an amended return for 2014 to claim $567 of the deductions. This is the deductions allocable to the foreign earned income ($9,500) multiplied by the includible portion of the foreign earned income ($6,300) and divided by the total foreign earned income for 2014 ($105,500).

Exemptions

You can claim an exemption for your nonresident alien spouse on your separate return, provided your spouse has no gross income for U.S. tax purposes and is not the dependent of another U.S. taxpayer.

You also can claim exemptions for individuals who qualify as your dependents. To be your dependent, the individual must be a U.S. citizen, U.S. national, U.S. resident alien, or a resident of Canada or Mexico for some part of the calendar year in which your tax year begins.

Children. Children usually are citizens or residents of the same country as their parents. If you were a U.S. citizen when your child was born, your child generally is a U.S. citizen. This is true even if the child's other parent is a nonresident alien, the child was born in a foreign country, and the child lives abroad with the other parent.

If you have a legally adopted child who is not a U.S. citizen, U.S. resident, or U.S. national, the child meets the citizen requirement if you are a U.S. citizen or U.S. national and the child lived with you as a member of your household all year.

Social security number. You must include on your return the social security number (SSN) of each dependent for whom you claim an exemption. To get a social security number for a dependent, apply at a Social Security office or U.S. consulate. You must provide original or certified copies of documents to verify the dependent's age, identity, and citizenship, and complete Form SS-5.

If you do not have an SSN for a child who was born in 2015 and died in 2015, attach a copy of the child's birth certificate to your tax return. Print "Died" in column (2) of line 6c of your Form 1040 or Form 1040A.

If your dependent is a nonresident alien who is not eligible to get a social security number, you must list the dependent's individual taxpayer identification number (ITIN) instead of an SSN. To apply for an ITIN, file Form W-7 with the IRS. It usually takes 6 to 10 weeks to get an

ITIN. Enter your dependent's ITIN wherever an SSN is requested on your tax return.

Additional information on obtaining an ITIN is available in the Instructions for Form W-7 and at *www.irs.gov/Individuals/Individual-Taxpayer-Identification-Number-ITIN*.

More information. For more information about exemptions, see Pub. 501.

Contributions to Foreign Charitable Organizations

If you make contributions directly to a foreign church or other foreign charitable organization, you generally cannot deduct them. Exceptions are explained under *Canadian, Mexican, and Israeli charities,* later.

You can deduct contributions to a U.S. organization that transfers funds to a charitable foreign organization if the U.S. organization controls the use of the funds by the foreign organization or if the foreign organization is just an administrative arm of the U.S. organization.

Canadian, Mexican, and Israeli charities. Under the income tax treaties with Canada, Mexico, and Israel, you may be able to deduct contributions to certain Canadian, Mexican, and Israeli charitable organizations. Generally, you must have income from sources in Canada, Mexico, or Israel, and the organization must meet certain requirements. See Pub. 597, Information on the United States-Canada Income Tax Treaty, and Pub. 526, Charitable Contributions, for more information.

Moving Expenses

If you moved to a new home in 2015 because of your job or business, you may be able to deduct the expenses of your move. Generally, to be deductible, the moving expenses must have been paid or incurred in connection with starting work at a new job location. See Pub. 521 for a complete discussion of the deduction for moving expenses and information about moves within the United States.

Foreign moves. A foreign move is a move in connection with the start of work at a new job location outside the United States and its possessions. A foreign move does not include a move back to the United States or its possessions.

Allocation of Moving Expenses

When your new place of work is in a foreign country, your moving expenses are directly connected with the income earned in that foreign country. If you exclude all or part of the income that you earn at the new location under the foreign earned income exclusion or the foreign housing exclusion, you cannot deduct the part of your moving expense that is allocable to the excluded income.

Also, you cannot deduct the part of the moving expense related to the excluded income for

a move from a foreign country to the United States if you receive a reimbursement that you are able to treat as compensation for services performed in the foreign country.

Year to which expense is connected. The moving expense is connected with earning the income (including reimbursements, as discussed in chapter 4 under *Reimbursement of moving expenses*) either entirely in the year of the move or in 2 years. It is connected with earning the income entirely in the year of the move if you qualify for the foreign earned income exclusion under the bona fide residence test or physical presence test for at least 120 days during that tax year.

If you do not qualify under either the bona fide residence test or the physical presence test for at least 120 days during the year of the move, the expense is connected with earning the income in 2 years. The moving expense is connected with the year of the move and the following year if the move is from the United States to a foreign country. The moving expense is connected with the year of the move and the preceding year if the move is from a foreign country to the United States.

Amount allocable to excluded income. To figure the amount of your moving expense that is allocable to your excluded foreign earned income (and not deductible), you must multiply your total moving expense deduction by a fraction. The numerator (top number) of the fraction is the total of your excluded foreign earned income and housing amounts for both years and the denominator (bottom number) of the fraction is your total foreign earned income for both years.

Example. On November 1, 2014, you transfer to Monaco. Your tax home is in Monaco, and you are a bona fide resident of Monaco for the entire tax year 2015. In 2014, you paid $6,000 for allowable moving expenses for your move from the United States to Monaco. You were fully reimbursed (under a nonaccountable plan) for these expenses in the same year. The reimbursement is included in your income. Your only other income for 2015 consists of $16,000 wages earned in 2014 after the date of your move, and $101,700 wages earned in Monaco for 2015.

Because you did not meet the bona fide residence test for at least 120 days during 2014, the year of the move, the moving expenses are for services you performed in both 2014 and the following year, 2015. Your total foreign earned income for both years is $123,700, consisting of $16,000 wages for 2014, $101,700 wages for 2015, and $6,000 moving expense reimbursement for both years.

You have no housing exclusion. The total amount you can exclude is $117,107, consisting of the $100,800 full-year exclusion for 2015 and a $16,307 part-year exclusion for 2014 ($99,200 times the fraction of 60 qualifying bona fide residence days over 365 total days in the year). To find the part of your moving expenses that is not deductible, multiply your $6,000 total expenses by the fraction $117,107 over $123,700. The result, $5,680, is your nondeductible amount.

You must report the full amount of the moving expense reimbursement in the year in which you received the reimbursement. In the preceding example, this year was 2014. You attribute the reimbursement to both 2014 and 2015 only to figure the amount of foreign earned income eligible for exclusion for each year.

Move between foreign countries. If you move between foreign countries, your moving expense is allocable to income earned in the year of the move if you qualified under either the bona fide residence test or the physical presence test for a period that includes at least 120 days in the year of the move.

New place of work in U.S. If your new place of work is in the United States, the deductible moving expenses are directly connected with the income earned in the United States. If you treat a reimbursement from your employer as foreign earned income (see the discussion in chapter 4), you must allocate deductible moving expenses to foreign earned income.

Storage expenses. These expenses are attributable to work you do during the year in which you incur the storage expenses. You cannot deduct the amount allocable to excluded income.

Moving Expense Attributable to Foreign Earnings in 2 Years

If your moving expense deduction is attributable to your foreign earnings in 2 years (the year of the move and the following year), you should request an extension of time to file your return for the year of the move until after the end of the second year. By then, you should have all the information needed to properly figure the moving expense deduction. See *Extensions* under *When To File and Pay* in chapter 1.

If you do not request an extension, you should figure the part of the moving expense that you cannot deduct because it is allocable to the foreign earned income you are excluding. You do this by multiplying the moving expense by a fraction, the numerator (top number) of which is your excluded foreign earned income for the year of the move, and the denominator (bottom number) of which is your total foreign earned income for the year of the move. Once you know your foreign earnings and exclusion for the following year, you must either:
- Adjust the moving expense deduction by filing an amended return for the year of the move, or
- Recapture any additional unallowable amount as income on your return for the following year.

If, after you make the final computation, you have an additional amount of allowable moving expense deduction, you can claim this only on an amended return for the year of the move. You cannot claim it on the return for the second year.

Forms To File

Report your moving expenses on Form 3903. Report your moving expense deduction on line 26 of Form 1040. If you must reduce your moving expenses by the amount allocable to excluded income (as explained later under *How To Report Deductions*), attach a statement to your return showing how you figured this amount.

For more information about figuring moving expenses, see Pub. 521.

Contributions to Individual Retirement Arrangements

Contributions to your individual retirement arrangements (IRAs) that are traditional IRAs or Roth IRAs are generally limited to the lesser of $5,500 ($6,500 if 50 or older) or your compensation that is includible in your gross income for the tax year. In determining compensation for this purpose, do not take into account amounts you exclude under either the foreign earned income exclusion or the foreign housing exclusion. Do not reduce your compensation by the foreign housing deduction.

If you are covered by an employer retirement plan at work, your deduction for your contributions to your traditional IRAs is generally limited based on your modified adjusted gross income. This is your adjusted gross income figured without taking into account the foreign earned income exclusion, the foreign housing exclusion, or the foreign housing deduction. Other modifications are also required. For more information on contributions to IRAs, see Pub. 590-A.

Taxes of Foreign Countries and U.S. Possessions

You can take either a credit or a deduction for income taxes paid to a foreign country or a U.S. possession. Taken as a deduction, foreign income taxes reduce your taxable income. Taken as a credit, foreign income taxes reduce your tax liability. You must treat all foreign income taxes the same way. If you take a credit for any foreign income taxes, you cannot deduct any foreign income taxes. However, you may be able to deduct other foreign taxes. See *Deduction for Other Foreign Taxes*, later.

There is no rule to determine whether it is to your advantage to take a deduction or a credit for foreign income taxes. In most cases, it is to your advantage to take foreign income taxes as a tax credit, which you subtract directly from your U.S. tax liability, rather than as a deduction in figuring taxable income. However, if foreign income taxes were imposed at a high rate and the proportion of foreign income to U.S. income is small, a lower final tax may result from deducting the foreign income taxes. In any event,

you should figure your tax liability both ways and then use the one that is better for you.

You can make or change your choice within 10 years from the due date for filing the tax return on which you are entitled to take either the deduction or the credit.

Foreign income taxes. These are generally income taxes you pay to any foreign country or possession of the United States.

Foreign income taxes on U.S. return. Foreign income taxes can only be taken as a credit on Form 1040, line 48, or as an itemized deduction on Schedule A. These amounts cannot be included as withheld income taxes on Form 1040, line 64.

Foreign taxes paid on excluded income. You cannot take a credit or deduction for foreign income taxes paid on earnings you exclude from tax under any of the following.
- Foreign earned income exclusion.
- Foreign housing exclusion.
- Possession exclusion.

If your wages are completely excluded, you cannot deduct or take a credit for any of the foreign taxes paid on your wages.

If only part of your wages is excluded, you cannot deduct or take a credit for the foreign income taxes allocable to the excluded part. You find the taxes allocable to your excluded wages by applying a fraction to the foreign taxes paid on foreign earned income received during the tax year. The numerator (top number) of the fraction is your excluded foreign earned income received during the tax year minus deductible expenses allocable to that income (not including the foreign housing deduction). The denominator (bottom number) of the fraction is your total foreign earned income received during the tax year minus all deductible expenses allocable to that income (including the foreign housing deduction).

If foreign law taxes both earned income and some other type of income and the taxes on the other type cannot be separated, the denominator of the fraction is the total amount of income subject to foreign tax minus deductible expenses allocable to that income.

 If you take a foreign tax credit for tax on income you could have excluded under your choice to exclude foreign earned income or your choice to exclude foreign housing costs, one or both of the choices may be considered revoked.

Credit for Foreign Income Taxes

If you take the foreign tax credit, you may have to file Form 1116 with Form 1040. Form 1116 is used to figure the amount of foreign tax paid or accrued that can be claimed as a foreign tax credit. Do not include the amount of foreign tax paid or accrued as withheld federal income taxes on Form 1040, line 64.

The foreign income tax for which you can claim a credit is the amount of legal and actual tax liability you pay or accrue during the year. The amount for which you can claim a credit is not necessarily the amount withheld by the foreign country. You cannot take a foreign tax credit for income tax you paid to a foreign country that would be refunded by the foreign country if you made a claim for refund.

Subsidies. If a foreign country returns your foreign tax payments to you in the form of a subsidy, you cannot claim a foreign tax credit based on these payments. This rule applies to a subsidy provided by any means that is determined, directly or indirectly, by reference to the amount of tax, or to the base used to figure the tax.

Some ways of providing a subsidy are refunds, credits, deductions, payments, or discharges of obligations. A credit is also not allowed if the subsidy is given to a person related to you, or persons who participated in a transaction or a related transaction with you.

Limit

The foreign tax credit is limited to the part of your total U.S. tax that is in proportion to your taxable income from sources outside the United States compared to your total taxable income. The allowable foreign tax credit cannot be more than your actual foreign tax liability.

Exemption from limit. You will not be subject to this limit and will not have to file Form 1116 if you meet all three of the following requirements.
- Your only foreign source income for the year is passive income (dividends, interest, royalties, etc.) that is reported to you on a payee statement (such as a Form 1099-DIV or 1099-INT).
- Your foreign taxes for the year that qualify for the credit are not more than $300 ($600 if you are filing a joint return) and are reported on a payee statement.
- You elect this procedure.

If you make this election, you cannot carry back or carry over any unused foreign tax to or from this year.

Separate limit. You must figure the limit on a separate basis with regard to "passive category income" and "general category income" (see the instructions for Form 1116).

Figuring the limit. In figuring taxable income in each category, you take into account only the amount that you must include in income on your federal tax return. Do not take any excluded amount into account.

To determine your taxable income in each category, deduct expenses and losses that are definitely related to that income.

Other expenses (such as itemized deductions or the standard deduction) not definitely related to specific items of income must be apportioned to the foreign income in each category by multiplying them by a fraction. The numerator (top number) of the fraction is your gross foreign income in the separate limit category. The denominator (bottom number) of the fraction is your gross income from all sources. For this purpose, gross income includes income that is excluded under the foreign earned

income provisions but does not include any other exempt income. You must use special rules for deducting interest expenses. For more information on allocating and apportioning your deductions, see Pub. 514.

Exemptions. Do not take the deduction for exemptions for yourself, your spouse, or your dependents in figuring taxable income for purposes of the limit.

Recapture of foreign losses. If you have an overall foreign loss and the loss reduces your U.S. source income (resulting in a reduction of your U.S. tax liability), you must recapture the loss in later years when you have taxable income from foreign sources. This is done by treating a part of your taxable income from foreign sources in later years as U.S. source income. This reduces the numerator of the limiting fraction and the resulting foreign tax credit limit.

Recapture of domestic losses. If you have an overall domestic loss (resulting in no U.S. tax liability), you cannot claim a foreign tax credit for taxes paid during that year. You must recapture the loss in later years when you have U.S. source taxable income. This is done by treating a part of your taxable income from U.S. sources in later years as foreign source income. This increases the numerator of the limiting fraction and the resulting foreign tax credit limit.

Foreign tax credit carryback and carryover. The amount of foreign income tax not allowed as a credit because of the limit can be carried back 1 year and carried forward 10 years.

More information on figuring the foreign tax credit can be found in Pub. 514.

Deduction for Foreign Income Taxes

Instead of taking the foreign tax credit, you can deduct foreign income taxes as an itemized deduction on Schedule A (Form 1040).

You can deduct only foreign income taxes paid on income that is subject to U.S. tax. You cannot deduct foreign taxes paid on earnings you exclude from tax under any of the following.
- Foreign earned income exclusion.
- Foreign housing exclusion.
- Possession exclusion.

Example. You are a U.S. citizen and qualify to exclude your foreign earned income. Your excluded wages in Country X are $70,000 on which you paid income tax of $10,000. You received dividends from Country X of $2,000 on which you paid income tax of $600.

You can deduct the $600 tax payment because the dividends relating to it are subject to U.S. tax. Because you exclude your wages, you cannot deduct the income tax of $10,000.

If you exclude only a part of your wages, see the earlier discussion under *Foreign taxes paid on excluded income.*

Deduction for Other Foreign Taxes

You can deduct real property taxes you pay that are imposed on you by a foreign country. You take this deduction on Schedule A (Form 1040). You cannot deduct other foreign taxes, such as personal property taxes, unless you incurred the expenses in a trade or business or in the production of income.

On the other hand, you generally can deduct personal property taxes when you pay them to U.S. possessions. But if you claim the possession exclusion, see Pub. 570.

The deduction for foreign taxes other than foreign income taxes is not related to the foreign tax credit. You can take deductions for these miscellaneous foreign taxes and also claim the foreign tax credit for income taxes imposed by a foreign country.

How To Report Deductions

If you exclude foreign earned income or housing amounts, how you show your deductions on your tax return and how you figure the amount allocable to your excluded income depends on whether the expenses are used in figuring adjusted gross income (Form 1040, line 38) or are itemized deductions.

If you have deductions used in figuring adjusted gross income, enter the total amount for each of these items on the appropriate lines and schedules of Form 1040. Generally, you figure the amount of a deduction related to the excluded income by multiplying the deduction by a fraction, the numerator of which is your foreign earned income exclusion and the denominator of which is your foreign earned income. Enter the amount of the deduction(s) related to excluded income on line 44 of Form 2555.

If you have itemized deductions related to excluded income, enter on Schedule A (Form 1040) only the part not related to excluded income. You figure that amount by subtracting from the total deduction the amount related to excluded income. Generally, you figure the amount that is related to the excluded income by multiplying the total deduction by a fraction, the numerator of which is your foreign earned income exclusion and the denominator of which is your foreign earned income. Attach a statement to your return showing how you figured the deductible amount.

Example 1. You are a U.S. citizen employed as an accountant. Your tax home is in Germany for the entire tax year. You meet the physical presence test. Your foreign earned income for the year was $126,000 and your investment income was $8,890. After excluding $100,800, your AGI is $34,090.

You had unreimbursed business expenses of $2,500 for travel and entertainment in earning your foreign income, of which $500 was for meals and entertainment. These expenses are deductible only as miscellaneous deductions on Schedule A (Form 1040). You also have $500 of miscellaneous expenses that are not related to your foreign income that you enter on line 23 of Schedule A.

You must fill out Form 2106. On that form, reduce your deductible meal and entertainment expenses by 50% ($250). You must reduce the remaining $2,250 of travel and entertainment expenses by 80% ($1,800) because you excluded 80% ($100,800/$126,000) of your foreign earned income. You carry the remaining total of $450 to line 21 of Schedule A. Add the $450 to the $500 that you have on line 23 and enter the total ($950) on line 24.

On line 26 of Schedule A, enter $682, which is 2% of your adjusted gross income of $34,090 (line 38, Form 1040) and subtract it from the amount on line 24.

Enter $268 on line 27 of Schedule A.

Example 2. You are a U.S. citizen, have a tax home in Spain, and meet the physical presence test. You are self-employed and personal services produce the business income. Your gross income was $120,444, business expenses $67,695, and net income (profit) $52,749. You choose the foreign earned income exclusion and exclude $100,800 of your gross income. Since your excluded income is 83.69% of your total income, 83.69% of your business expenses are not deductible. Report your total income and expenses on Schedule C (Form 1040). On Form 2555 you will show the following:

- Line 20a, $120,444, gross income,
- Lines 42 and 43, $100,800, foreign earned income exclusion, and
- Line 44, $56,654 (83.69% × $67,695) business expenses attributable to the exclusion.

 In this situation (Example 2), you cannot use Form 2555-EZ since you had self-employment income and business expenses.

Example 3. Assume in *Example 2* that both capital and personal services combine to produce the business income. No more than 30% of your net income, or $15,825, assuming that this amount is a reasonable allowance for your services, is considered earned and can be excluded. Your exclusion of $15,825 is 13.14% of your gross income ($15,825 ÷ $120,444). Because you excluded 13.14% of your net income, $8,895 (.1314 x $67,695) of your business expenses is attributable to the excluded income and is not deductible.

Example 4. You are a U.S. citizen, have a tax home in Brazil, and meet the physical presence test. You are self-employed and both capital and personal services combine to produce business income. Your gross income was $146,000, business expenses were $172,000, and your net loss was $26,000. A reasonable allowance for the services you performed for the business is $77,000. Because you incurred a net loss, the earned income limit of 30% of your net profit does not apply. The $77,000 is foreign earned income. If you choose to exclude the $77,000, you exclude 52.74% of your gross income ($77,000 ÷ $146,000), and 52.74% of your business expenses ($90,713) is

attributable to that income and is not deductible. Show your total income and expenses on Schedule C (Form 1040). On Form 2555, exclude $77,000 and show $90,713 on line 44. Subtract line 44 from line 43, and enter the difference as a negative (in parentheses) on line 45. Because this amount is negative, enter it as a positive (no parentheses) on line 21, Form 1040, and combine it with your other income to arrive at total income on line 22 of Form 1040.

 In this situation (Example 4), you would probably not want to choose the foreign earned income exclusion if this was the first year you were eligible. If you had chosen the exclusion in an earlier year, you might want to revoke the choice for this year. To do so would mean that you could not claim the exclusion again for the next 5 tax years without IRS approval. See Choosing the Exclusion *in chapter 4.*

Example 5. You are a U.S. citizen, have a tax home in Panama, and meet the bona fide residence test. You have been performing services for clients as a partner in a firm that provides services exclusively in Panama. Capital investment is not material in producing the partnership's income. Under the terms of the partnership agreement, you are to receive 50% of the net profits. The partnership received gross income of $248,000 and incurred operating expenses of $102,250. Of the net profits of $145,750, you received $72,875 as your distributive share.

You choose to exclude $100,800 of your share of the gross income. Because you exclude 80% ($108,000 ÷ $126,000) of your share of the gross income, you cannot deduct $40,900, 80% of your share of the operating expenses (.80 × $51,125). Report $72,875, your distributive share of the partnership net profit, on Schedule E (Form 1040), Supplemental Income and Loss. On Form 2555, show $100,800 on line 42 and show $40,900 on line 44. Your exclusion on Form 2555 is $59,900.

 In this situation (Example 5), you cannot use Form 2555-EZ since you had earned income other than salaries and wages and you had business expenses.

6.

Tax Treaty Benefits

Topics
This chapter discusses:

- Some common tax treaty benefits,
- How to get help in certain situations, and

- How to get copies of tax treaties.

Useful Items
You may want to see:

Publication

❑ **597** Information on the United States—Canada Income Tax Treaty

❑ **901** U.S. Tax Treaties

See chapter 7 for information about getting these publications.

Purpose of Tax Treaties

The United States has tax treaties or conventions with many countries. See Table 6-1 at the end of this chapter for a list of these treaties.

Under these treaties and conventions, citizens and residents of the United States who are subject to taxes imposed by the foreign countries are entitled to certain credits, deductions, exemptions, and reductions in the rate of taxes of those foreign countries. If a foreign country with which the United States has a treaty imposes a tax on you, you may be entitled to benefits under the treaty.

Treaty benefits generally are available to residents of the United States. They generally are not available to U.S. citizens who do not reside in the United States. However, certain treaty benefits and safeguards, such as the nondiscrimination provisions, are available to U.S. citizens residing in the treaty countries. U.S. citizens residing in a foreign country also may be entitled to benefits under that country's tax treaties with third countries.

Certification of U.S. residency. Use Form 8802, Application for United States Residency Certification, to request certification of U.S. residency for purposes of claiming benefits under a tax treaty. Certification can be requested for the current and any prior calendar years.

 You should examine the specific treaty articles to find if you are entitled to a tax credit, tax exemption, reduced rate of tax, or other treaty benefit or safeguard.

Common Benefits

Some common tax treaty benefits are explained below. The credits, deductions, exemptions, reductions in rate, and other benefits provided by tax treaties are subject to conditions and various restrictions. Benefits provided by certain treaties are not provided by others.

Personal service income. If you are a U.S. resident who is in a treaty country for a limited number of days in the tax year and you meet certain other requirements, the payment you receive for personal services performed in that country may be exempt from that country's income tax.

Professors and teachers. If you are a U.S. resident, the payment you receive for the first 2 or 3 years that you are teaching or doing research in a treaty country may be exempt from that country's income tax.

Students, trainees, and apprentices. If you are a U.S. resident, amounts you receive from the United States for study, research, or business, professional and technical training may be exempt from a treaty country's income tax.

Some treaties exempt grants, allowances, and awards received from governmental and certain nonprofit organizations. Also, under certain circumstances, a limited amount of pay received by students, trainees, and apprentices may be exempt from the income tax of many treaty countries.

Pensions and annuities. If you are a U.S. resident, nongovernment pensions and annuities you receive may be exempt from the income tax of treaty countries.

Most treaties contain separate provisions for exempting government pensions and annuities from treaty country income tax, and some treaties provide exemption from the treaty country's income tax for social security payments.

Investment income. If you are a U.S. resident, investment income, such as interest and dividends, that you receive from sources in a treaty country may be exempt from that country's income tax or taxed at a reduced rate.

Several treaties provide exemption for capital gains (other than from sales of real property in most cases) if specified requirements are met.

Tax credit provisions. If you are a U.S. resident who receives income from or owns capital in a foreign country, you may be taxed on that income or capital by both the United States and the treaty country.

Most treaties allow you to take a credit against or deduction from the treaty country's taxes based on the U.S. tax on the income.

Nondiscrimination provisions. Most U.S. tax treaties provide that the treaty country cannot discriminate by imposing more burdensome taxes on U.S. citizens who are residents of the treaty country than it imposes on its own citizens in the same circumstances.

Saving clauses. U.S. treaties contain saving clauses that provide that the treaties do not affect the U.S. taxation of its own citizens and residents. As a result, U.S. citizens and residents generally cannot use the treaty to reduce their U.S. tax liability.

However, most treaties provide exceptions to saving clauses that allow certain provisions of the treaty to be claimed by U.S. citizens or residents. It is important that you examine the applicable saving clause to determine if an exception applies.

More information on treaties. Pub. 901 contains an explanation of treaty provisions that apply to amounts received by teachers, students, workers, and government employees and pensioners who are alien nonresidents or residents of the United States. Since treaty provisions generally are reciprocal, you usually can substitute "United States" for the name of the treaty country whenever it appears, and vice versa when "U.S." appears in the treaty exemption discussions in Pub. 901.

Pub. 597 contains an explanation of a number of frequently-used provisions of the United States–Canada income tax treaty.

Competent Authority Assistance

If you are a U.S. citizen or resident alien, you can request assistance from the U.S. competent authority if you think that the actions of the United States, a treaty country, or both, cause or will cause a tax situation not intended by the treaty between the two countries. You should read any treaty articles, including the mutual agreement procedure article, that apply in your situation.

The U.S. competent authority cannot consider requests involving countries with which the United States does not have a tax treaty.

A complete listing of the information that must be included with the request can be found in Revenue Procedure 2015-40 available at *www.irs.gov/irb/2015-35_IRB/ar10.html*.

Your request for competent authority consideration should be addressed to:

Deputy Commissioner (International)
Large Business and International Division
Internal Revenue Service
1111 Constitution Avenue, NW
Washington, DC 20224
SE:LB:IN:ADCI:TAIT:M4-365
(Attention: TAIT)

Obtaining Copies of Tax Treaties

Table 6-1 lists those countries with which the United States has income tax treaties. This table is updated through October 31, 2015.

You can get complete information about treaty provisions from the taxing authority in the country from which you receive income or from the treaty itself. You can obtain the text of most U.S. treaties at IRS.gov. Enter "Tax treaties" in the search box. Click "United States Income Tax Treaties–A to Z."

If you have questions about a treaty you can visit *www.irs.gov/Individuals/International-Taxpayers/Tax-Treaties*.

Table 6–1. **List of Tax Treaties** (Updated through October 31, 2015)

Country	General Effective Date [1]	Country	General Effective Date [1]
Australia	Dec. 1, 1983	Japan	Jan. 1, 2005
Protocol	Jan. 1, 2004	Kazakhstan	Jan. 1, 1996
Austria	Jan. 1, 1999	Korea, South	Jan. 1, 1980
Bangladesh	Jan. 1, 2007	Latvia	Jan. 1, 2000
Barbados	Jan. 1, 1984	Lithuania	Jan. 1, 2000
Protocol	Jan. 1, 1994	Luxembourg	Jan. 1, 2001
Protocol	Jan. 1, 2005	Malta	Jan. 1, 2011
Belgium	Jan. 1, 2008	Mexico	Jan. 1, 1994
Bulgaria	Jan. 1, 2009	Protocol	Oct. 26,1995
Canada[2]	Jan. 1, 1985	Protocol	Jan. 1, 2004
Protocol	Jan. 1, 1996	Morocco	Jan. 1, 1981
Protocol	Dec.16, 1997	Netherlands	Jan. 1, 1994
Protocol	Jan. 1, 2009	Protocol	Jan. 1, 2005
China, People's Republic of	Jan. 1, 1987	New Zealand	Jan. 1, 1984
Commonwealth of Independent States[3]	Jan. 1, 1976	Protocol	Jan. 1, 2011
Cyprus	Jan. 1, 1986	Norway	Jan. 1, 1971
Czech Republic	Jan. 1, 1993	Protocol	Jan. 1, 1982
Denmark	Jan. 1, 2001	Pakistan	Jan. 1, 1959
Protocol	Jan. 1, 2008	Philippines	Jan. 1, 1983
Egypt	Jan. 1, 1982	Poland	Jan. 1, 1974
Estonia	Jan. 1, 2000	Portugal	Jan. 1, 1996
Finland	Jan. 1, 1991	Romania	Jan. 1, 1974
Protocol	Jan. 1, 2008	Russia	Jan. 1, 1994
France	Jan. 1, 1996	Slovak Republic	Jan. 1, 1993
Protocol	Jan. 1, 2007	Slovenia	Jan. 1, 2002
Protocol	Jan. 1, 2010	South Africa	Jan. 1, 1998
Germany	Jan. 1, 1990	Spain	Jan. 1, 1991
Protocol	Jan. 1, 2008	Sri Lanka	Jan. 1, 2004
Greece	Jan. 1, 1953	Sweden	Jan. 1, 1996
Hungary	Jan. 1, 1980	Protocol	Jan. 1, 2007
Iceland	Jan. 1, 2009	Switzerland	Jan. 1, 1998
India	Jan. 1, 1991	Thailand	Jan. 1, 1998
Indonesia	Jan. 1, 1990	Trinidad and Tobago	Jan. 1, 1970
Protocol	Feb. 1, 1997	Tunisia	Jan. 1, 1990
Ireland	Jan. 1, 1998	Turkey	Jan. 1, 1998
Amending Convention	Sep. 1, 2000	Ukraine	Jan. 1, 2001
Israel	Jan. 1, 1995	United Kingdom	Jan. 1, 2004
Italy	Jan. 1, 2010	Venezuela	Jan. 1, 2000
Jamaica	Jan. 1, 1982		

[1] The general effective date of the treaty is when a treaty enters into force. However, there are often separate effective dates for taxes withheld at source and for all other taxes, and in some instances taxpayers may be able to apply an existing treaty for an additional year. Check the treaty and/or protocol for effective dates for specific types of income.

[2] Information on the treaty can be found in Publication 597, *Information on the United States—Canada Income Tax Treaty.*

[3] The U.S.-U.S.S.R. income tax treaty applies to the countries of Armenia, Azerbaijan, Belarus, Georgia, Kyrgyzstan, Moldova, Tajikistan, Turkmenistan, and Uzbekistan.

7.

How To Get Tax Help

Assistance for overseas taxpayers is available in the U.S and certain foreign locations.

Taxpayer Assistance Inside the United States

If you have questions about a tax issue, need help preparing your tax return, or want to download free publications, forms, or instructions, go to IRS.gov and find resources that can help you right away.

Preparing and filing your tax return. Find free options to prepare and file your return on IRS.gov or in your local community if you qualify.

- Go to IRS.gov and click on the Filing tab to see your options.
- Enter "Free File" in the search box to see whether you can use brand-name software to prepare and *e-file* your federal tax return for free.
- Enter "VITA" in the search box, download the free IRS2Go app, or call 1-800-906-9887 to find the nearest Volunteer Income Tax Assistance or Tax Counseling for the Elderly (TCE) location for free tax preparation.
- Enter "TCE" in the search box, download the free IRS2Go app, or call 1-888-227-7669 to find the nearest Tax Counseling for the Elderly location for free tax preparation.

The Volunteer Income Tax Assistance (VITA) program offers free tax help to people who generally make $54,000 or less, persons with disabilities, the elderly, and limited-English-speaking taxpayers who need help preparing their own tax returns. The Tax Counseling for the Elderly (TCE) program offers free tax help for all taxpayers, particularly those who are 60 years of age and older. TCE volunteers specialize in answering questions about pensions and retirement-related issues unique to seniors.

 Getting answers to your tax law questions. On IRS.gov get answers to your tax questions anytime, anywhere.

- Go to *www.irs.gov/Help-&-Resources* for a variety of tools that will help you with your taxes.
- Enter "ITA" in the search box on IRS.gov for the Interactive Tax Assistant, a tool that will ask you questions on a number of tax law topics and provide answers. You can print the entire interview and the final response.
- Enter "Pub 17" in the search box on IRS.gov to get Pub. 17, Your Federal

Income Tax for Individuals, which features details on tax-saving opportunities, 2015 tax changes, and thousands of interactive links to help you find answers to your questions.

- Additionally, you may be able to access tax law information in your electronic filing software.

Tax forms and publications. You can download or print all of the forms and publications you may need on *www.irs.gov/formspubs*. Otherwise, you can go to *www.irs.gov/orderforms* to place an order and have forms mailed to you. You should receive your order within 10 business days.

Direct deposit. The fastest way to receive a tax refund is by combining direct deposit and IRS *e-file*. Direct deposit securely and electronically transfers your refund directly into your financial account. Eight in 10 taxpayers use direct deposit to receive their refund. The majority of refunds are received within 21 days or less.

Getting a transcript or copy of a return.

- Go to IRS.gov and click on "Get Transcript of Your Tax Records" under "Tools."
- Call the transcript toll-free line at 1-800-908-9946.
- Mail Form 4506-T or Form 4506T-EZ (both available on IRS.gov).

Using online tools to help prepare your return. Go to IRS.gov and click on the Tools bar to use these and other self-service options.

- The *Earned Income Tax Credit Assistant* determines if you are eligible for the EIC.
- The *Online EIN Application* helps you get an employer identification number.
- The *IRS Withholding Calculator* estimates the amount you should have withheld from your paycheck for federal income tax purposes.
- The *Electronic Filing PIN Request* helps to verify your identity when you do not have your prior year AGI or prior year self-selected PIN available.
- The *First Time Homebuyer Credit Account Look-up* tool provides information on your repayments and account balance.

For help with the alternative minimum tax, go to IRS.gov/AMT.

Understanding identity theft issues.

- Go to *www.irs.gov/uac/Identity-Protection* for information and videos.
- If your SSN has been lost or stolen or you suspect you are a victim of tax-related identity theft, visit *www.irs.gov/identitytheft* to learn what steps you should take.

Checking on the status of a refund.

- Go to *www.irs.gov/refunds*.
- Download the free IRS2Go app to your smart phone and use it to check your refund status.
- Call the automated refund hotline at 1-800-829-1954.

Making a tax payment. The IRS uses the latest encryption technology so electronic payments are safe and secure. You can make elec-

tronic payments online, by phone, or from a mobile device. Paying electronically is quick, easy, and faster than mailing in a check or money order. Go to *www.irs.gov/payments* to make a payment using any of the following options.

- *IRS Direct Pay* (for individual taxpayers who have a checking or savings account).
- **Debit or credit card** (approved payment processors online or by phone).
- **Electronic Funds Withdrawal** (available during *e-file*).
- **Electronic Federal Tax Payment System** (best option for businesses; enrollment required).
- **Check or money order**.
- IRS2Go provides access to mobile-friendly payment options like IRS Direct Pay, offering you a free, secure way to pay directly from your bank account. You can also make debit or credit card payments through an approved payment processor. Simply download IRS2Go from Google Play, the Apple App Store, or the Amazon Appstore, and make your payments anytime, anywhere.

What if I can't pay now? Click on the "Pay Your Tax Bill" icon on IRS.gov for more information about these additional options.

- Apply for an *online payment agreement* to meet your tax obligation in monthly installments if you cannot pay your taxes in full today. Once you complete the online process, you will receive immediate notification of whether your agreement has been approved.
- An offer in compromise allows you to settle your tax debt for less than the full amount you owe. Use the *Offer in Compromise Pre-Qualifier* to confirm your eligibility.

Checking the status of an amended return. Go to IRS.gov and click on the Tools tab and then *Where's My Amended Return?*

Understanding an IRS notice or letter. Enter "Understanding your notice" in the search box on IRS.gov to find additional information about your IRS notice or letter.

Visiting the IRS. Locate the nearest Taxpayer Assistance Center using the Office Locator tool on IRS.gov. Enter "office locator" in the search box. Or choose the "Contact Us" option on the IRS2Go app and search Local Offices. Before you visit, use the Locator tool to check hours and services available.

Watching IRS videos. The IRS Video portal *www.irsvideos.gov* contains video and audio presentations for individuals, small businesses, and tax professionals. You'll find video clips of tax topics, archived versions of panel discussions and Webinars, and audio archives of tax practitioner phone forums.

Getting tax information in other languages. For taxpayers whose native language is not English, we have the following resources available.

1. Taxpayers can find information on IRS.gov in the following languages.

a. *Spanish.*

b. *Chinese.*

c. *Vietnamese.*

d. *Korean.*

e. *Russian.*

2. The IRS Taxpayer Assistance Centers provide over-the-phone interpreter service in over 170 languages, and the service is available free to taxpayers.

The Taxpayer Advocate Service Is Here To Help You

What is the Taxpayer Advocate Service?

The Taxpayer Advocate Service (TAS) is an *independent* organization within the Internal Revenue Service that helps taxpayers and protects taxpayer rights. Our job is to ensure that every taxpayer is treated fairly and that you know and understand your rights under the *Taxpayer Bill of Rights*.

What Can the Taxpayer Advocate Service Do For You?

We can help you resolve problems that you can't resolve with the IRS. And our service is free. If you qualify for our assistance, you will be assigned to one advocate who will work with you throughout the process and will do everything possible to resolve your issue. TAS can help you if:

- Your problem is causing financial difficulty for you, your family, or your business,
- You face (or your business is facing) an immediate threat of adverse action, or
- You've tried repeatedly to contact the IRS but no one has responded, or the IRS hasn't responded by the date promised.

How Can You Reach Us?

We have offices *in every state, the District of Columbia, and Puerto Rico*. Your local advocate's number is in your local directory and at *www.taxpayeradvocate.irs.gov*. You can also call us at 1-877-777-4778.

How Can You Learn About Your Taxpayer Rights?

The Taxpayer Bill of Rights describes ten basic rights that all taxpayers have when dealing with the IRS. Our Tax Toolkit at *www.taxpayeradvocate.irs.gov* can help you understand *what these rights mean to you* and how they apply. These are *your* rights. Know them. Use them.

How Else Does the Taxpayer Advocate Service Help Taxpayers?

TAS works to resolve large-scale problems that affect many taxpayers. If you know of one of these broad issues, please report it to us at *www.irs.gov/sams*.

Low Income Taxpayer Clinics

Low Income Taxpayer Clinics (LITCs) serve individuals whose income is below a certain level and need to resolve tax problems such as audits, appeals, and tax collection disputes. Some clinics can provide information about taxpayer rights and responsibilities in different languages for individuals who speak English as a second language. To find a clinic near you, visit *www.irs.gov/litc* or see IRS Publication 4134, *Low Income Taxpayer Clinic List*.

Taxpayer Assistance Outside the United States

 If you are outside the United States, you can call 267-941-1000 (English-speaking only). This number is not toll free.

 If you wish to write instead of calling, please address your letter to:

Internal Revenue Service
International Accounts
Philadelphia, PA 19255-0725
U.S.A.

Additional contacts for taxpayers who live outside the United States are available at *www.irs.gov/uac/Contact-My-Local-Office-Internationally*.

Taxpayer Advocate Service. If you live outside of the United States, you can call the Taxpayer Advocate at (787) 522-8601 in English or (787) 522-8600 in Spanish. You can contact the Taxpayer Advocate at:

Internal Revenue Service
Taxpayer Advocate Service
City View Plaza, 48 Carr 165,
Guaynabo, P.R. 00968-8000

You can call the Taxpayer Advocate toll-free at 1-877-777-4778. For more information on the Taxpayer Advocate Service and contacts if you are outside of the United States go to *www.irs.gov/Advocate/Local-Taxpayer-Advocate/Contact-Your-Local-Taxpayer-Advocate*.

Questions and Answers

This section answers tax-related questions commonly asked by taxpayers living abroad.

Filing Requirements—Where, When, and How

1) When are U.S. income tax returns due?

Generally, for calendar year taxpayers, U.S. income tax returns are due on April 15. If you are a U.S. citizen or resident and both your tax home and your abode are outside the United States and Puerto Rico on the regular due date, an automatic extension is granted to June 15 for filing the return. Interest will be charged on any tax due, as shown on the return, from April 15.

2) I am going abroad this year and expect to qualify for the foreign earned income exclusion. How can I secure an extension of time to file my return, when should I file my return, and what forms are required?

a) You should file Form 2350 by the due date of your return to request an extension of time to file. Form 2350 is a special form for those U.S. citizens or residents abroad who expect to qualify for the foreign earned income exclusion or the housing exclusion or deduction under either the bona fide residence test or physical presence test and would like to have an extension of time to delay filing until after they have qualified.

b) If the extension is granted, you should file your return after you qualify, but by the approved extension date.

c) You must file your Form 1040 with Form 2555 (or Form 2555-EZ).

3) My entire income qualifies for the foreign earned income exclusion. Must I file a tax return?

Generally, yes. Every U.S. citizen or resident who receives income must file a U.S. income tax return unless total income without regard to the foreign earned income exclusion is below an amount based on filing status. The income levels for filing purposes are discussed under *Filing Requirements* in chapter 1.

4) I was sent abroad by my company in November of last year. I plan to secure an extension of time on Form 2350 to file my tax return for last year because I expect to qualify for the foreign earned income exclusion under the physical presence test. However, if my company recalls me to the United States before the end of the qualifying period and I find I will not qualify for the exclusion, how and when should I file my return?

If your regular filing date has passed, you should file a return, Form 1040, as soon as possible for last year. Include a statement with this return noting that you have returned to the United States and will not qualify for the foreign earned income exclusion. You must report your worldwide income on the return. If you paid a foreign tax on the income earned abroad, you may be able to either deduct this tax as an itemized deduction or claim it as a credit against your U.S. income tax.

However, if you pay the tax due after the regular due date, interest will be charged from the regular due date until the date the tax is paid.

5) I am a U.S. citizen and have no taxable income from the United States, but I have substantial income from a foreign source. Am I required to file a U.S. income tax return?

Yes. All U.S. citizens and resident aliens are subject to U.S. tax on their worldwide income. If you paid taxes to a foreign government on income from sources outside the United States, you may be able to claim a foreign tax credit against your U.S. income tax liability for the foreign taxes paid. Form 1116 is used to figure the allowable credit.

6) I am a U.S. citizen who has retired, and I expect to remain in a foreign country. Do I have any further U.S. tax obligations?

Your U.S. tax obligation on your income is the same as that of a retired person living in the United States. (See the discussion on filing requirements in chapter 1 of this publication.)

7) I have been a bona fide resident of a foreign country for over 5 years. Is it necessary for me to pay estimated tax?

U.S. taxpayers overseas have the same requirements for paying estimated tax as those in the United States. See the discussion under *Estimated Tax* in chapter 1.

Overseas taxpayers should not include in their estimated income any income they receive that is, or will be, exempt from U.S. taxation.

Overseas taxpayers can deduct their estimated housing deduction in figuring their estimated tax.

The first installment of estimated tax is due on April 15 of the year for which the income is earned.

8) Will a check payable in foreign currency be acceptable in payment of my U.S. tax?

Generally, only U.S. currency is acceptable for payment of income tax. However, if you are a Fulbright grantee, see *Fulbright Grant* in chapter 1.

9) I have met the test for physical presence in a foreign country and am filing returns for 2 years. Must I file a separate Form 2555 (or Form 2555-EZ) with each return?

Yes. A Form 2555 (or Form 2555-EZ) must be filed with each Form 1040 tax return on which the benefits of income earned abroad are claimed.

10) Does a Form 2555 (or 2555-EZ) with a Schedule C or Form W-2 attached constitute a return?

No. The Form 2555 (or 2555-EZ), Schedule C, and Form W-2 are merely attachments and do not relieve you of the requirement to file a Form 1040 to show the sources of income reported and the exclusions or deductions claimed.

11) On Form 2350, Application for Extension of Time To File U.S. Income Tax Return, I stated that I would qualify for the foreign earned income exclusion under the physical presence test. If I qualify under the bona fide residence test, can I file my return on that basis?

Yes. You can claim the foreign earned income exclusion and the foreign housing exclusion or deduction under either test as long as you meet the requirements. You are not bound by the test indicated in the application for extension of time. You must be sure, however, that you file the Form 1040 by the date approved on Form 2350, since a return filed after that date may be subject to a failure to file penalty.

If you will not qualify under the bona fide residence test until a date later than the extension granted under the physical presence rule, apply for a new extension to a date 30 days beyond the date you expect to qualify as a bona fide resident.

12) I am a U.S. citizen who worked in the United States for 6 months last year. I accepted employment overseas in July of last year and expect to qualify for the foreign earned income exclusion. Should I file a return and pay tax on the income earned in the United States during the first 6 months and then, when I qualify, file another return covering the last 6 months of the year?

No. You have the choice of one of the following two methods of filing your return:

a) You can file your return when due under the regular filing rules, report all your income without excluding your foreign earned income, and pay the tax due. After you have qualified for the exclusion, you can file an amended return, Form 1040X, accompanied by Form 2555 (or 2555-EZ), for a refund of any excess tax paid.

b) You can postpone the filing of your tax return by applying on Form 2350 for an extension of time to file to a date 30 days beyond the date you expect to qualify under either the bona fide residence test or the physical presence test, then file your return reflecting the exclusion of foreign earned income. This allows you to file only once and saves you from paying the tax and waiting for a refund. However, interest is charged on any tax due on the postponed tax return, but interest is not paid on refunds paid within 45 days after the return is filed. If you have moving expenses that are for services performed in two years, you can be granted an extension until after the end of the second year.

13) I am a U.S. citizen. I have lived abroad for a number of years and recently realized that I should have been filing U.S. income tax returns. How do I correct this oversight in not having filed returns for these years?

File the late returns as soon as possible, stating your reason for filing late. For advice on filing the returns, you should contact an Internal Revenue Service representative.

14) In 2010, I qualified to exclude my foreign earned income, but I did not claim this exclusion on the return I filed in 2011. I paid all outstanding taxes with the return. Can I file a claim for refund now?

It is too late to claim this refund since a claim for refund must be filed within 3 years from the date the return was filed or 2 years from the date the tax was paid, whichever is later. A return filed before the due date is considered filed on the due date.

Meeting the Requirements of Either the Bona Fide Residence Test or the Physical Presence Test

1) I recently came to Country X to work for the Orange Tractor Co. and I expect to be here for 5 or 6 years. I understand that upon the completion of 1 full year I will qualify for an exclusion or deduction under the bona fide residence test. Is this correct?

Not necessarily. The law provides that to qualify under this test for the foreign earned income exclusion, the foreign housing exclusion, or the foreign housing deduction, a person must be a bona fide resident of a foreign country or countries for an uninterrupted period which includes an entire taxable year.

If, like most U.S. citizens, you file your return on a calendar year basis, the taxable year referred to in the law would be from January 1 to December 31 of any particular year. Unless you established residence in Country X on January 1, it would be more than 1 year before you would be a bona fide resident of a foreign country. Once you have completed your qualifying period, however, you are entitled to exclude the income or to claim the housing exclusion or deduction from the date you established bona fide residence.

2) I understand the physical presence test to be simply a matter of being physically present in a foreign country for at least 330 days within 12 consecutive months; but what are the criteria of the bona fide residence test?

To be a bona fide resident of a foreign country, you must show that you entered a foreign country intending to remain there for an indefinite or prolonged period and, to that end, you are making your home in that country. Consideration is given to the type of quarters occupied, whether your family went with you, the type of visa, the employment agreement, and any other factor pertinent to show whether your stay in the foreign country is indefinite or prolonged.

To claim the foreign earned income exclusion or foreign housing exclusion or deduction under this test, the period of foreign residence must include 1 full tax year (usually January 1 – December 31), but once you meet this time requirement, you figure the exclusions and the deduction from the date the residence actually began.

3) To meet the qualification of "an uninterrupted period which includes an entire taxable year," do I have to be physically present in a foreign country for the entire year?

No. Uninterrupted refers to the bona fide residence proper and not to the physical presence of the individual. During the period of bona fide residence in a foreign country, even during the first full year, you can leave the country for brief and temporary trips back to the United States or elsewhere for vacation, or even for business. To preserve your status as a bona fide resident of a foreign country, you must have a clear intention of returning from those trips, without unreasonable delay, to your foreign residence.

4) I am a U.S. citizen and during 2014 was a bona fide resident of Country X. On January 15, 2015, I was notified that I was to be assigned to Country Y. I was recalled to New York for 90 days orientation and then went to Country Y, where I have been since. Although I was not in Country Y on January 1, I was a bona fide resident of Country X and was in Country Y on December 31, 2015. My family remained in Country X until completion of the orientation period, and my household goods were shipped directly to my new post. Am I a bona fide resident of a foreign country for 2015, or must I wait for the entire year of 2016 to become one?

Because you did not break your period of foreign residence, you would continue to be a bona fide resident of a foreign country for 2015.

5) Due to illness, I returned to the United States before I completed my qualifying period to claim the foreign earned income exclusion. Can I figure the exclusion for the period I resided abroad?

No. You are not entitled to any exclusion of foreign earned income since you did not complete your qualifying period under either the bona fide residence test or physical presence test. If you paid foreign tax on the income earned abroad, you may be able to claim that tax as a deduction or as a credit against your U.S. tax.

6) Can a resident alien of the United States qualify for an exclusion or deduction under the bona fide residence test or the physical presence test?

Resident aliens of the United States can qualify for the foreign earned income exclusion, the foreign housing exclusion, or the foreign housing deduction if they meet the requirements of the physical presence test. Resident aliens who are citizens or nationals of a country with which the United States has an income tax treaty in effect also can qualify under the bona fide residence test.

7) On August 13 of last year I left the United States and arrived in Country Z to work for the Gordon Manufacturing Company. I expected to be able to exclude my foreign earned income under the physical presence test because I planned to be in Country Z for at least 1 year. However, I was reassigned back to the United States and left Country Z on July 1 of this year. Can I exclude any of my foreign earned income?

No. You cannot exclude any of the income you earned in Country Z because you were not in a foreign country for at least 330 full days as required under the physical presence test.

Foreign Earned Income

1) I am an employee of the U.S. Government working abroad. Can all or part of my government income earned abroad qualify for the foreign earned income exclusion?

No. The foreign earned income exclusion applies to your foreign earned income. Amounts paid by the United States or its agencies to their employees are not treated, for this purpose, as foreign earned income.

2) I qualify for the foreign earned income exclusion under the bona fide residence test. Does my foreign earned income include my U.S. dividends and the interest I receive on a foreign bank account?

No. The only income that is foreign earned income is income from the performance of personal services abroad. Investment income is not earned income. However, you must include it in gross income reported on your Form 1040.

3) My company pays my foreign income tax on my foreign earnings. Is this taxable compensation?

Yes. The amount is compensation for services performed. The tax paid by your company should be reported on Form 1040, line 7, and on Form 2555, Part IV, line 22(f) (or on Form 2555-EZ, Part IV, line 17).

4) I live in an apartment in a foreign city for which my employer pays the rent. Should I include in my income the cost to my employer ($1,200 a month) or the fair market value of equivalent housing in the United States ($800 a month)?

You must include in income the fair market value (FMV) of the facility provided, where it is provided. This will usually be the rent your employer pays. Situations when the FMV is not included in income are discussed in chapter 4 under *Exclusion of Meals and Lodging*.

5) My U.S. employer pays my salary into my U.S. bank account. Is this income considered earned in the United States or is it considered foreign earned income?

If you performed the services to earn this salary outside the United States, your salary is considered earned abroad. It does not matter that you are paid by a U.S. employer or that your salary is deposited in a U.S. bank account in the United States. The source of salary, wages, commissions, and other personal service income is the place where you perform the services.

6) What is considered a foreign country?

For the purposes of the foreign earned income exclusion and the foreign housing exclusion or deduction, any territory under the sovereignty of a country other than the United States is a foreign country. Possessions of the United States are not treated as foreign countries.

7) What is the source of earned income?

The source of earned income is the place where the work or personal services that produce the income are performed. In other words, income received for work in a foreign country has its source in that country. The foreign earned income exclusion and the foreign housing exclusion or deduction are limited to earned income from sources within foreign countries.

Foreign Earned Income Exclusion

1) I qualify for the foreign earned income exclusion and earned more than $100,800 during 2015. Am I entitled to the maximum $100,800 exclusion?

Not necessarily. Although you qualify for the foreign earned income exclusion, you may not have met either the bona fide residence test or the physical presence test for your entire tax year. If you did not meet either of these tests for your entire tax year, you must prorate the maximum exclusion based on the number of days that you did meet either test during the year.

2) How do I qualify for the foreign earned income exclusion?

To be eligible, you must have a tax home in a foreign country and be a U.S. citizen or resident alien. You must be either a bona fide resident of a foreign country or countries for an uninterrupted period that includes an entire tax year, or you must be physically present in a foreign country or countries for at least 330 full days during any period of 12 consecutive months. U.S. citizens may qualify under either test. The physical presence test applies to all resident aliens, while the bona fide residence test applies to resident aliens who are citizens or nationals of a country with which the United States has an income tax treaty in effect.

Your tax home must be in the foreign country or countries throughout your period of residence or presence. For this purpose, your period of physical presence is the 330 full days during which you are present in a foreign country, not the 12 consecutive months during which those days occur.

3) Is it true that my foreign earned income exclusion cannot exceed my foreign earned income?

Yes. The amount of the exclusion is limited each year to the amount of your foreign earned income after reducing that income by the foreign housing exclusion. The foreign earned income must be earned during the part of the tax year that you have your tax home abroad and meet either the bona fide residence test or the physical presence test.

4) My wife and I are both employed, reside together, and file a joint return. We meet the qualifications for claiming the foreign earned income exclusion. Do we each figure a separate foreign earned income exclusion and foreign housing exclusion?

You figure your foreign earned income exclusion separately since you both have foreign earned income. The amount of the exclusion

for each of you cannot exceed your separate foreign earned incomes.

You must figure your housing exclusion jointly. See *Married Couples* in chapter 4 for further details.

Exemptions and Dependency Allowances

1) I am a U.S. citizen married to a nonresident alien who has no income from U.S. sources. Can I claim an exemption for my spouse on my U.S. tax return?

Yes. If you file a joint return, you can claim an exemption for your nonresident alien spouse. If you do not file a joint return, you can claim an exemption for your nonresident alien spouse only if your spouse has no income from sources within the United States and is not the dependent of another U.S. taxpayer.

You must use the married filing separately column in the Tax Table or section C of the Tax Computation Worksheet, unless you qualify as a head of household. (Also see Question 12 under *General Tax Questions*, later.)

A U.S. citizen or resident alien married to a nonresident alien also can choose to treat the nonresident alien as a U.S. resident for all federal income tax purposes. This allows you to file a joint return, but also subjects the alien's worldwide income to U.S. income tax.

2) I support my parents who live in Italy. I am sure that I provide the bulk of their support. Can I claim exemptions for them?

It depends on whether they are U.S. citizens or U.S residents. If your parents are not U.S. citizens or U.S. residents, you cannot claim exemptions for them even if you provide most of their support. To qualify as a dependent, a person generally must be either a U.S. citizen, U.S. national, U.S. resident alien, or a resident of Canada or Mexico for some part of the tax year. The other tests of dependency also must be met.

3) Should I prorate my own personal exemption and the exemptions for my spouse and dependents, since I expect to exclude part of my income?

No. Do not prorate exemptions. Claim the full amount for each exemption permitted.

Social Security and Railroad Retirement Benefits

1) Are U.S. social security benefits taxable?

Benefits received by U.S. citizens and resident aliens may be taxable, depending on the total amount of income and the filing status of the taxpayer. Under certain treaties, U.S. social security benefits are exempt from U.S. tax if taxed by the country of residence.

Benefits similar to social security received from other countries by U.S. citizens or residents may be taxable. (Refer to our tax treaties with various countries for any benefit granted by the treaty.)

2) As a U.S. citizen or resident alien, how do I figure the amount of my U.S. social security benefits to include in gross income?

See Pub. 915, Social Security and Equivalent Railroad Retirement Benefits, to figure if any of your benefits are includible in income.

3) How are railroad retirement benefits taxed?

The part of a tier 1 railroad retirement benefit that is equivalent to the social security benefit you would have been entitled to receive if the railroad employee's work had been covered under the social security system rather than the railroad retirement system is treated the same as a social security benefit, discussed above.

The other part of a tier 1 benefit that is not considered a social security equivalent benefit is treated like a private pension or annuity, as are tier 2 railroad retirement benefits. Pensions and annuities are explained in chapter 4 under *Earned and Unearned Income*. Vested dual benefits and supplemental annuities are also treated like private pensions, but are fully taxable.

The proper amounts of the social security equivalent part of tier 1 benefits and any special guaranty benefits are shown on the Form RRB-1099, Payments by the Railroad Retirement Board, that you receive from the Railroad Retirement Board. The taxable amounts of the non-social security equivalent part of tier 1, tier 2, vested dual benefits, and supplemental annuities are shown on the Form RRB-1099-R,

Annuities or Pensions by the Railroad Retirement Board, that you receive from the Railroad Retirement Board.

Social Security Tax and Self-Employment Tax

1) I am a minister with earned income from abroad and expect to qualify for the foreign earned income exclusion. How do I pay my self-employment tax?

File a Form 1040 with Schedule SE and Form 2555. Figure your self-employment tax on Schedule SE and enter it on Form 1040 as the tax due with the return.

2) Because I expect to qualify for the foreign earned income exclusion, I have requested and received an extension of time until January 30, 2017, to file my 2015 return. However, since I will be paying self-employment tax on my spouse's income, should I file a 2015 return when due, pay the self-employment tax, and then file another return when I qualify for the exclusion?

No. You do not need to file a 2015 Form 1040 (the regular income tax return) when due if you have received an extension. Instead, you should pay enough estimated tax to cover the self-employment tax and any income tax that would be due after taking out the amount of excludable income.

Income Tax Withholding

1) How can I get my employer to stop withholding federal income taxes from wages while I am overseas and eligible for the foreign earned income exclusion?

File a statement in duplicate with your employer stating that withholding should be reduced because you meet the bona fide residence test or physical presence test. See also the following question.

2) Does the Internal Revenue Service provide forms to be used by employees requesting employers to stop withholding income tax from wages they expect to be excluded as income earned abroad?

Yes. Form 673 is a sample statement that can be used by individuals who expect to qualify for the foreign earned income exclusion under the bona fide residence test or the physical presence test. A copy of this form is displayed in chapter 2.

3) I am a U.S. citizen residing overseas, and I receive dividend and interest income from U.S. sources from which tax is being withheld at a rate of 30%. How can I have this situation corrected?

File Form W-9 (indicating that you are a U.S. citizen) with the withholding agents who are paying you the dividends and interest. This is their authority to stop withholding the 30% income tax at the source on payments due you.

4) As a U.S. citizen receiving dividend and interest income from the United States from which tax has been withheld, do I report the net dividend and interest income on my return, or do I report the gross amount and take credit for the tax withheld?

You must report the gross amount of the income received and take a tax credit for the tax withheld. This is to your advantage since the tax withheld is deducted in full from the tax due. It is also advisable to attach a statement to your return explaining this tax credit so there will be no question as to the amount of credit allowable.

Deductions

1) Can I claim a foreign tax credit even though I do not itemize deductions?

Yes. You can claim the foreign tax credit even though you do not itemize deductions.

2) I had to pay customs duty on a few things I brought back with me from Europe last summer. Can I include customs fees with my other deductible taxes?

No. Customs duties, like federal excise taxes, are not deductible.

3) What types of foreign taxes are deductible?

Generally, real estate and foreign income taxes are deductible as itemized deductions. Foreign income taxes are deductible only if you do not claim the foreign tax credit. Foreign income taxes paid on excluded income are not deductible as an itemized deduction.

Note. Foreign income taxes are usually claimed under the credit provisions, if they apply, because this is more advantageous in most cases.

4) I rented an apartment in the United Kingdom and had to pay a local tax called a "general rates" tax, which is based on occupancy of the apartment. Can I deduct this tax as a foreign real estate tax?

No. This tax does not qualify as a real estate tax since it is levied on the occupant of the premises rather than on the owner of the property.

Scholarship and Fellowship Grantees

1) I am a Fulbright grantee. What documentation must I attach to my return?

a) There are no special tax forms for Fulbright grantees. File on a regular Form 1040.

b) If you claim exemption as a scholarship or fellowship grantee, submit brochures and correspondence describing the grant and your duties.

c) If you are located in a foreign country and wish to pay tax in foreign currency, you should submit a certified statement showing that you were a Fulbright grantee and at least 70% of the grant was paid in nonconvertible foreign currency.

2) I taught and lectured abroad under taxable grants. What expenses can I deduct?

You may be able to deduct your travel, meals, and lodging expenses if you are temporarily absent from your regular place of employment. For more information about deducting travel, meals, and lodging expenses, get Pub. 463, Travel, Entertainment, Gift, and Car Expenses.

General Tax Questions

1) Can Internal Revenue Service personnel recommend tax practitioners who prepare returns?

No. IRS employees are not permitted to recommend tax practitioners who prepare income tax returns.

2) I just filed my return. How do I check the status of my refund?

See *Refund Information* in your tax return instructions.

3) I have not received my refund from last year's return. Can I claim the credit against this year's tax?

No. That would cause problems to both years' returns. If your last year's refund is overdue, call or write the IRS. If you write to the IRS, be sure to include your social security number (or individual taxpayer identification number) in the letter.

4) I forgot to include interest income when I filed my return last week. What should I do?

To correct a mistake of this sort, you should prepare Form 1040X. Include the omitted interest income, refigure the tax, and send the form as soon as possible along with any additional tax due to the Internal Revenue Service Center where you filed your return. Use Form 1040X to correct an individual Form 1040 income tax return filed for any year for which the period of limitation has not expired (usually 3 years after the due date of the return filed, or 2 years after the tax was paid, whichever is later).

5) I am a U.S. citizen and, because I expect to qualify for the foreign earned income exclusion, all my foreign income (which consists solely of salary) will be exempt from U.S. tax. Do I get any tax benefit from income tax I paid on this salary to a foreign country during the tax year?

No. You cannot take either a tax credit or a tax deduction for foreign income taxes paid on income that is exempt from U.S. tax because of the foreign earned income exclusion.

6) I am a U.S. citizen stationed abroad. I made a personal loan to a nonresident alien who later went bankrupt. Can I claim a bad debt loss for this money?

Yes. The loss should be reported as a short-term capital loss on Schedule D (Form 1040). You have the burden of proving the validity of the loan, the subsequent bankruptcy, and the recovery or nonrecovery from the loan.

7) With which countries does the United States have tax treaties?

Table 6-1, at the end of chapter 6, lists those countries with which the United States has income tax treaties.

8) I am a retired U.S. citizen living in Europe. My only income is from U.S. sources on which I pay U.S. taxes. I am taxed on the same income in the foreign country where I reside. How do I avoid double taxation?

If you reside in a country that has an income tax treaty with the United States, the treaty will generally contain provisions to eliminate double taxation. Many treaties will provide reduced rates for various types of income. Treaties often provide reciprocal credits in one country for the tax paid to the other country. Nontreaty countries, depending on their laws, may give the same type of credit.

If double taxation with a treaty country exists and you cannot resolve the problem with the tax authorities of the foreign country, you can contact the U.S. competent authority for assistance. See chapter 6 for information on requesting consideration.

9) My total income after claiming the foreign earned income and housing exclusions consists of $5,000 taxable wages. Am I entitled to claim the earned income credit?

No. If you claim the foreign earned income exclusion, the foreign housing exclusion, or the foreign housing deduction, you cannot claim the earned income credit.

10) I am claiming the foreign earned income credit. Can I take the additional child tax credit?

No. You cannot take the additional child tax credit if you claim either the foreign earned income or foreign housing exclusion, or the foreign housing deduction.

11) Last May my employer transferred me to our office in Puerto Rico. I understand that my salary earned in Puerto Rico is tax exempt. Is this correct?

As long as your employer is not the U.S. Government, all income from sources within Puerto Rico is exempt from U.S. tax if you are a bona fide resident of Puerto Rico during the entire tax year. The income you received from Puerto Rican sources the year you moved to Puerto Rico is not exempt. The tax paid to Puerto Rico in the year you moved to Puerto Rico can be claimed as a foreign tax credit on Form 1116.

12) I am a U.S. citizen married to a nonresident alien. Can I qualify to use the head of household tax rates?

Yes. Although your nonresident alien spouse cannot qualify you as a head of household, you may qualify if you maintain a household for a qualifying child or other relative.

If your spouse was a nonresident alien at any time during the year and you do not choose to treat your nonresident alien spouse as a resident alien, then you are treated as unmarried for head of household purposes. You must have another qualifying person and meet the other tests to be eligible to file as head of household. You can use the head of household column in the Tax Table or Section D of the Tax Computation Worksheet.

It may be advantageous to choose to treat your nonresident alien spouse as a U.S. resident and file a joint income tax return. Once you make the choice, however, you must report the worldwide income of both yourself and your spouse.

For more information on head of household filing status, get Pub. 501, Exemptions, Standard Deduction, and Filing Information.

Penalties and Interest

1) Does the June 15 extended due date for filing my return because both my tax home and my abode are outside the United States and Puerto Rico on the regular due date relieve me from having to pay interest on tax not paid by April 15?

No. An extension, whether an automatic extension or one requested in writing, does not relieve you of the payment of interest on the tax due as of April 15 following the year for which the return is filed. The interest should be included in your payment.

2) If I wait to file my return until I qualify for the foreign earned income exclusion, I will be charged interest on the U.S. tax I will owe. To avoid being charged interest, can I file my return on time, reporting only my taxable income, excluding my salary for services abroad that will be exempt after I have met the qualifications?

No. If you file a return before you qualify for the exclusion, you must report all income, including all income for services performed abroad, and pay tax on all of it. After you meet the qualifications, you can file a claim for refund by excluding the income earned abroad. If you defer the filing of your return, you can avoid interest on tax due on your return to be filed by paying the tax you estimate you will owe with your request for an extension of time to file on Form 2350, or by paying enough estimated tax to cover any tax that you expect will be due on the return.

■

Index

To help us develop a more useful index, please let us know if you have ideas for index entries. See "Comments and Suggestions" in the "Introduction" for the ways you can reach us.

www.ingramcontent.com/pod-product-compliance
Lightning Source LLC
Chambersburg PA
CBHW080644190526
45169CB00009B/3494